TARASOFF AND BEYOND:
Legal and Clinical Considerations In the Treatment of Life-Endangering Patients

Third Edition

Leon VandeCreek, PhD, ABPP

School of Professional Psychology
Wright State University

Samuel Knapp, EdD

Pennsylvania Psychological Association
Harrisburg, Pennsylvania

Professional Resource Press
Sarasota, FL

Published by
Professional Resource Press
(An imprint of the Professional Resource Exchange, Inc.)
Post Office Box 15560
Sarasota, FL 34277-1560

Printed in the United States of America

This publication is sold with the understanding that the Publisher is not engaged in rendering professional services. If legal, psychological, medical, accounting, or other expert advice or assistance is sought or required, the reader should seek the services of a competent professional.

The copy editor for this book was Judith Warinner, the managing editor was Debbie Fink, and the production coordinator was Laurie Girsch.

The views expressed in this guide do not necessarily represent those of the Pennsylvania Psychological Association.

Library of Congress Cataloging-in-Publication Data

VandeCreek, Leon.
    Tarasoff and beyond : legal and clinical considerations in the treatment of
life-endangering patients / Leon VandeCreek, Samuel Knapp.–3rd ed.
        p. cm. -- (Practitioner's resource series)
    Includes bibliographical references.
    ISBN 1-56887-070-1 (alk. paper)
        1. Psychotherapists--Legal status, laws, etc.--United States. 2. Insane, Criminal and
dangerous--Legal status, laws, etc.--United States. 3. Confidential
communications--Physicians--United States. 4. Disclosure of information--Law and
legislation--United States. 5. Medical ethics--United States. I. Knapp, Samuel. II. Title.
III. Series.

KF3828 V36 2001
344.73'0412--dc21

                                                          2001031844

SERIES PREFACE

As a publisher of books, audio- and videotapes, and continuing education programs, the Professional Resource Press strives to provide mental health professionals with highly applied resources that can be used to enhance clinical skills and expand practical knowledge.

All of the titles in the Practitioner's Resource Series are designed to provide important new information on topics of vital concern to psychologists, clinical social workers, marriage and family therapists, psychiatrists, and other mental health professionals.

Although the focus and content of each book in this series will be quite different, there will be notable similarities:

1. Each title in the series will address a timely topic of critical clinical importance.

2. The target audience for each title will be practicing mental health professionals. Our authors were chosen for their ability to provide concrete "how-to-do-it" guidance to colleagues who are trying to increase their competence in dealing with complex clinical problems.

3. The information provided in these books will represent "state-of-the-art" information and techniques derived from both clinical experience and empirical research. Each of these guidebooks will include references and resources for those who wish to pursue more advanced study of the discussed topics.

4. The authors will provide numerous case studies, specific recommendations for practice, and the types of "nitty-gritty" details that clinicians need before they can incorporate new concepts and procedures into their practices.

We feel that one of the unique assets of Professional Resource Press is that all of its editorial decisions are made by mental health professionals. The publisher, all editorial consultants, and all reviewers are practicing psychologists, marriage and family therapists, clinical social workers, and psychiatrists.

If there are other topics you would like to see addressed in this series, please let me know.

Lawrence G. Ritt, Publisher

ABSTRACT

The ethical, legal, and clinical problems in treating life-endangering patients were highlighted in the case of *Tarasoff v. Regents of the University of California* (1976). In that case, the California Supreme Court concluded that in some instances the protection of confidentiality in psychotherapy must give way to the right to safety of potential victims of violence from patients. Although *Tarasoff* is the most famous court case dealing with life-endangering patients, other court cases and statutory rules also regulate and provide guidance for assessment and treatment of these patients.

This guidebook discusses the *Tarasoff* decision and subsequent related court decisions and their ethical, legal, and clinical implications. The guidebook focuses primarily on the management of homicidal patients. In addition, the authors extend their discussion to the management of HIV-positive patients, suicidal patients, and child-abusing parents. Other topics are discussed to a lesser extent, including impaired drivers, patient disclosures of past crimes, and psychotherapist liability for wrongful civil commitments and releases.

The guidebook is not intended to be a comprehensive treatment manual, but it does discuss clinical interventions and considerations that will minimize liability risks, and, at the same time, provide quality treatment for patients.

In this third edition, the authors provide information and references to the most recent research findings and court cases.

TABLE OF CONTENTS

THE DUTY TO WARN OR PROTECT
WITH DANGEROUS PATIENTS *(Continued)*

TARASOFF
AND BEYOND:
Legal and Clinical Considerations
In the Treatment of
Life-Endangering Patients*

Third Edition

INTRODUCTION

Even though the rate of homicides in the United States is dropping, the societal concern about violence has not diminished, especially in the wake of highly publicized incidents in schools and places of work. Psychotherapists are often required to respond to situations in which serious threats of violence have been made.

Few situations are as stressful as those dealing with life-endangering patients. Psychotherapists may be called to the emergency room of a hospital late at night to evaluate a prospective patient accompanied by the police or relatives. The examination may be made under difficult circumstances. The police may present their concerns in a demanding manner, and the relatives may lie blatantly to rid themselves of the patient. In addition, the patient may be angry, confused, or afraid to communicate.

---

*The authors present information on the legal and clinical obligations of psychotherapists when dealing with life-endangering patients. We are not, however, offering legal advice or clinical guidance on any particular case. Psychotherapists who encounter patients who threaten to harm themselves or others need to learn the applicable case or statutory laws in their particular state.

For the sake of consistency we have used the word "patient" throughout the book even though some psychotherapists may prefer to use the word "client." At times we comment on the need to refer to physicians. The same legal obligations would apply if psychotherapists were referring the patient to an advance nurse practitioner or other health professional licensed as a psycho-pharmacologist.

In another context, the psychotherapist may be working with a voluntary outpatient, trying to defuse hostile and aggressive feelings and fantasies. The patient's anger or disorganization may become so severe that the psychotherapist may fear that a life may be endangered. When working with life-endangering patients, psychotherapists sometimes need to change roles, from an ally trying to activate the healthy aspects of the person to an agent of social control who determines that an intended victim must be warned, or that the patient must submit to an evaluation for an involuntary commitment.

In one sense, the most dangerous patients are the easiest to evaluate. The dangerousness of their acts and the degree of mental disorganization leave no doubt as to the proper decision. Other decisions are harder. When do threats become so severe that it is necessary to warn the intended victim? When does a suicidal gesture become severe enough to qualify as a suicidal act? How long can a person go without eating before it qualifies as neglect of self?

No psychotherapist, no matter how competent, can make these decisions with complete accuracy and foresight. Despite their extensive study of psychopathology, psychotherapists have limited ability to predict dangerousness. They may find themselves in a double bind. The failure to warn an intended victim may mean that a life is endangered. Conversely, that warning may alienate the patient from psychotherapy and increase the very danger that the psychotherapist was trying to avert.

ETHICAL ISSUES IN THE DUTY TO WARN OR PROTECT

Although this book focuses on legal and clinical considerations, we urge psychotherapists to consider the ethical or moral implications of their decision making. All competent psychotherapists feel a moral imperative to promote the welfare of their patients (beneficence), or at least to avoid harming them (nonmaleficence). Typically this is done through adherence to two other moral principles: respect for patient autonomy and fidelity or faithfulness to the foundations of the psychotherapeutic relationship, which includes adherence to the general principle to respect patient confidentiality. According to principle-based ethics, the general rule is that psychotherapists and other moral agents should follow these principles that are *prima facie* (moral obligations on their face; Beauchamp & Childress, 1994).

In the ordinary course of treatment, these moral principles do not conflict. However, these moral principles are not absolute and may be overridden in unusual situations if they conflict with another moral principle. When psychotherapists believe it is necessary to infringe upon one moral principle in an effort to adhere to another one, they should attempt to minimize the harm to the offended moral principle.

For example, psychotherapists generally show respect for patient autonomy by acknowledging the patient's control over the direction and major events of psychotherapy. However, under rare circumstances, such as when patients present an imminent danger of harm to themselves, psychotherapists may temporarily invoke the principle of beneficence to override (or "trump") the principles of respect for patient autonomy and fidelity to the confidentiality typically found in the psychotherapeutic relationship. Even when respect for patient autonomy and fidelity are trumped, it is still desirable to minimize the infringement of the patients' autonomy and to involve them as much as possible in deciding on the intervention to reduce the likelihood of self-harm. Similarly it is desirable to minimize the infringement of the patients' confidentiality by involving them as much as possible on what information is essential to convey. If the desired intervention requires notifying the spouse of the patient, then the psychotherapist can, for example, ask the patient, "How should we go about informing your spouse?" "Do you want to be present when I share the information about your needs?"

The same conflict may occur when a patient makes a credible threat to harm an identifiable third party. If no other clinical intervention can diffuse the danger, then the psychotherapist may decide to warn the identifiable victim. Again, even when respect for patient autonomy is trumped, it is desirable to minimize the infringement of autonomy and to involve the patient as much as possible in selecting the intervention designed to diffuse the danger. Fortunately, good ethical decision making is typically consistent with good clinical and legal decision making. Psychotherapists who act with beneficence and with respect for patient autonomy will almost always be meeting their legal responsibilities. Sometimes a particular state statute may require psychotherapists to warn (or conversely to refrain from warning), despite their belief that such an action (or inaction) would harm the patient or society. In such a situation, ethics will conflict with the law. Such occasions are rare and good clinical skills and creative clinical decision making can usually eliminate the apparent forced choice between obeying one's conscience and obeying the law. Nonetheless, clinicians should be aware that at times such a forced choice may be unavoidable.

The only advice we can offer for such situations is for psychotherapists to be prepared for them: know the state's law, have a ready network of valued consultants for difficult situations, and consider all decisions carefully.

THE PURPOSE OF THIS BOOK

This book is intended to help psychotherapists to consider legal and clinical factors when dealing with dangerous patients. We will review the *Tarasoff* case, subsequent representative cases dealing with the threat of harm to an identifiable third party, and legal standards when dealing with suicidal patients, child abuse, elder abuse, and impaired drivers. We also offer some basic clinical suggestions when dealing with life-endangering patients. Finally, we address issues of risk management, self-protection, and self-care.

Our goal is to help psychotherapists to fulfill their legal obligations when treating patients who threaten to harm themselves or others. In the course of doing so, we have found it helpful to present details on certain cases to illustrate judicial reasoning in the context of real-life situations. However, this book is not intended to be a detailed legal treatise and some technicalities of professional liability are presented in an abbreviated form.

THE DUTY TO WARN OR PROTECT WITH DANGEROUS PATIENTS

The issues surrounding the treatment of dangerous persons were highlighted in 1976 when the California Supreme Court concluded that psychotherapists have a duty to protect potential victims from dangerous patients (*Tarasoff v. Regents of the University of California*, 1976). A few commentators and therapists welcomed the court's conclusion as an endorsement of their current practices or ethical standards (e.g., Leonard, 1977). Nevertheless, many psychotherapists were shocked, angered, and frightened by the court's entry into the sphere of professional judgment.

The courts have been reluctant to enter the domain of professional practices, preferring to defer to the experts in those fields. The *Tarasoff* court concluded, however, that it had to enter the mental health field to correct an imbalance between the rights of psychotherapy patients to confidentiality and the rights of potential victims to safety from assault by these patients.

Subsequent court decisions in California and in other jurisdictions have sometimes clarified and sometimes muddied the issues. Nonetheless, it is possible to glean some general principles from these court cases, which together have forced the mental health professions to address the legal and clinical problems of treating life-endangering patients. In addition, numerous state legislatures have passed "duty to protect or warn" statutes that specify what psychotherapists must, must not, or may do when faced with dangerous patients.

Because this area of law is ever changing in the United States and Canada, we will not review every state statute or the case law from state Supreme Courts. There can be no substitute for keeping abreast of the laws in one's own state. Nonetheless, we will make general comments about the nature of the duties identified in those statutes and court cases. Our discussion of the duty to warn or protect starts with the *Tarasoff* case.

THE FACTS OF THE TARASOFF CASE

Prosenjit Poddar was born in Bengal, India, into the Harijan ("untouchable") caste. In September 1967, he entered the University of California at Berkeley as a graduate student and took up residence in the International House. In the fall of 1968, he attended folk-dancing classes at the International House, where he met and fell in love with a young American woman, Tatiana (Tanya) Tarasoff. Poddar persisted in courting Tarasoff, and he apparently misinterpreted her friendliness (including a New Year's Eve kiss) as a sign of deep affection and commitment. However, Tanya did not return his affections. She told him that she was interested in other men and did not want an intimate relationship with him.

Poddar underwent a severe emotional crisis after Tanya rebuffed him. He neglected his appearance, health, and studies. He often stayed alone, spoke disjointedly, and wept. He saw Tanya only occasionally during the spring of 1969. At times he tape-recorded parts of these conversations (apparently without her knowledge) to figure out why she did not return his love.

During the summer of 1969, Tanya went to Brazil and Poddar's emotional health began to improve. At the suggestion of a friend, Poddar sought mental health treatment at the Cowell Memorial Hospital, an affiliate of the University of California at Berkeley. He was initially interviewed by a psychiatrist and then started psychotherapy with a psychologist, Dr. Lawrence Moore.

During the session of August 18, 1969, Poddar confided to Moore his intent to kill Tanya when she returned from Brazil. Moore took the threats seriously. On August 20th, he consulted his superiors within the department of psychiatry. They agreed that Poddar should be involuntarily committed to a psychiatric hospital. Moore then asked the campus police to pick up Poddar and to proceed with commitment procedures. Moore stated that he would follow up the conversation with a letter of diagnosis.

In his letter to the campus police, Moore stated that Poddar was undergoing an acute and severe paranoid schizophrenic reaction and that he was a danger to others. Moore also stated that Poddar appeared rational at times, but quite psychotic at other times.

The campus police officers detained Poddar and talked to him. They did not commit him, however, because he appeared rational and promised to avoid Tanya. After the commitment attempt failed, Poddar discontinued therapy. Subsequently, Dr. Harvey Powelson, the director of the department of psychiatry, learned of the foiled arrangement to commit Poddar. He requested that the police chief return Moore's letters, ordered Moore to destroy his therapy notes, and instructed him to make no further attempts to commit Poddar.

The attempt to commit Poddar occurred only 2 months after the enactment of California's new commitment law. Consequently, neither the mental health professionals nor the police were experienced with the procedures required by the new commitment law. They also may have been uncertain about how the courts would interpret the new law. In fact, according to the new law, the city police, not the university police, should have picked up Poddar and transported him to a medical facility for an emergency psychiatric evaluation.

That fall, Tanya returned from Brazil, unaware of the danger to her. Meanwhile, Poddar persuaded her brother to share an apartment with him only a block away from Tanya's residence. In October 1969, Poddar went to Tanya's house to speak to her. Tanya refused to speak with him, but Poddar insisted. Tanya screamed, whereupon Poddar shot her with a pellet gun. Tanya fled the house, but Poddar apprehended her and repeatedly and fatally stabbed her with a kitchen knife. Poddar then returned to Tanya's house and called the police.

At the trial, Poddar's attorneys argued a defense of diminished capacity. They produced a psychologist and three psychiatrists who stated that Poddar had paranoid schizophrenia and could not have harbored malice of forethought at the time of the murder. In contrast, the prosecution-appointed psychiatrist held that Poddar was only schizoid, and that his mental state would make a charge of first- or second-degree murder appropriate. The Superior Court of Alameda County, California, convicted Poddar of second-degree murder.

The verdict, however, was reversed because the judge erred in his instructions to the jury. Poddar was released and returned to India. The last information on Poddar was a letter in which he stated that he was happily married (Stone, 1976).

THE TARASOFF *DECISION*

While the state was pursuing the criminal case, Tanya's parents initiated a wrongful-death suit against the Regents of the University of California, the psychologist and psychiatrists, and the police officers who were involved in the treatment of Poddar and the abortive attempt to commit him. The suit fueled a national debate concerning the limits of confidentiality with life-endangering patients.

The civil *Tarasoff* case was determined twice. The first *Tarasoff* decision in 1974 articulated a duty to warn. This decision led to so much controversy that, in an unusual move, the California Supreme Court agreed to re-review the case. In the second decision in 1976, the court modified its reasoning in reaching its decision. After the second decision was issued, the first decision lost any binding authority even in California. All subsequent references to *Tarasoff* refer to the second decision of 1976.

Tatiana Tarasoff's parents brought suit against the University of California and its employees on two major grounds: the failure to commit Poddar and the failure to warn Tanya of her peril. The defendants countered both charges. They argued that the California statutes protected them from liability for the failure to commit. Also, they argued that they should not have had to warn Tanya because predictions of dangerousness are too difficult to make with reasonable accuracy, and such warnings would have violated the confidentiality necessary for an effective psychotherapeutic relationship.

The court did not hold the defendants liable for failure to commit Poddar. They cited the relevant California statute that exempts public employees from liabilities for injuries resulting from decisions to release mental patients.

The court did, however, assess liability for the failure to warn Tarasoff of the danger to her. The decision was based, to a large extent, on the affirmative duty to act that arises out of the "special relationship" between a psychotherapist and a patient.

According to the common law, an individual usually has no duty to control the behavior of another to protect a third party. Nevertheless, once a "special relationship" has been established, the law may require affirmative obligations. These socially recognized relationships, such as parent to child or possessor of land to renter, imply a legal duty to attempt to protect others from harm, or to warn them of potential harm. For example, parents must protect their children, and physicians must protect the public by reporting the existence of a contagious disease.

Furthermore, custodians of patients in psychiatric or similar institutions have a duty to protect or warn third persons about dangerous patients. In several court cases (e.g., *Fair v. United States,* 1956; *Underwood v. United States,* 1966), hospitals or doctors in their employ were found liable for failure to warn murder victims of the dangerousness of released mental patients. In this regard, *Tarasoff* provided nothing new in the area of tort liability. The court merely applied inpatient tort law to an outpatient setting.

The court acknowledged some validity in the defendants' argument that dangerousness is hard to predict, but they ruled that difficulty in determining dangerousness does not remove the obligation of psychotherapists to protect others when such a determination is made. The court also rejected the contention that the provisions of the new commitment law prevented the defendants from disclosing information to the intended victim. The new commitment law delineated several exceptions to confidentiality, but it did not include warning potential victims as an exception. The court, however, held that the law only covers information acquired in the involuntary commitment of patients or acquired by employees at state and county hospitals. Other mental health professionals do not fall under the confidentiality provisions of the law.

The court also recognized that psychotherapy requires confidentiality to be effective. Justice Tobriner, writing for the majority opinion, stated, however:

> Public policy favoring protection of the confidential character of the patient-psychotherapist communications must yield to the extent to which disclosure is essential to avert danger to others since the protective privilege ends when the public peril begins. (pp. 334-337)

Because the *Tarasoff* decision has been subject to many misinterpretations, it is important to know what the *Tarasoff* court did not say. The court did not require psychotherapists to issue a warning every time a patient talks about an urge or fantasy to harm someone. On the contrary, the court stated, "A therapist should not be encouraged routinely to reveal such threats . . . unless such disclosure is necessary to avert danger to others" (p. 347). The court did not require psychotherapists to interrogate their clients or to conduct independent investigations when the identity of the victim is unknown. Rather, the duty to protect arises only when the victim has been identified or could be identified upon "a moment's reflection" (p. 345, fn 11). Finally, the court did not specify that warning the intended victim was the only required response when danger arises. On the contrary, the court stated that the "discharge of such duty may require the therapist to take one or more of various steps, depending on the nature of the case, including warning the intended victim" (p. 334). The therapist may initiate an involuntary commitment, notify the police, modify the treatment, or take other steps to deter the violence.

DISSENTING OPINIONS

The *Tarasoff* decision included a dissent by Justice Clark. Clark disagreed with the interpretation given to the application of the confidentiality sections of the state's commitment law. He believed that this law did apply to the mental health professionals involved, and that it prevented them from disclosing information. In addition to the alleged statutory misinterpretation found in the majority decision, Justice Clark stated that the decision was also poor public policy. "While offering virtually no benefit to society, such a duty will frustrate psychiatric treatment, invade fundamental patient rights and increase violence" (p. 358).

Justice Mosk also wrote a separate opinion in which he agreed in part and disagreed in part with the majority decision. Justice Mosk concurred in the result in this case because the "defendant therapists did in fact predict that Poddar would kill and were therefore negligent in failing to warn of that danger" (p. 353). The major point in his dissent concerned the standards the court used to judge the failure to predict a patient's violence. The majority held that the psychotherapists were required to adhere to the "standards of the profession" in predicting danger. Mosk asked, "What standards?" He noted that psychotherapists have no unique ability to predict danger and have been "incredibly inaccurate" in their predictions. Instead of adhering to the standards of the profession, Mosk wrote:

> I would restructure the rule designed by the majority to eliminate all reference to conformity to standards of the profession in predicting violence. If a psychiatrist does in fact predict violence, then a duty to warn arises. (p. 354)

LEGAL BACKGROUND ON THE
DUTY TO WARN OR PROTECT

Many psychotherapists resented the "new" legal intrusions into clinical practice. However, a study of the background of American common law shows that the "duty to protect" (*Tarasoff* doctrine) is not new. Rather, it is part of a legal tradition that has developed over many years. The only thing unique about *Tarasoff* is that it applied old legal principles regarding tort liability and negligence to a new context (Beigler, 1984).

Anglo-American law distinguishes between injuries arising out of an action ("misfeasance") and injuries arising out of nonaction ("nonfeasance"). According to traditional law, parties could be held responsible for injuries arising out of misfeasance, that is, injuries caused by their actions. They could not, however, be held responsible for injuries arising out of nonfeasance (Kamenar, 1984).

According to this distinction, no person is required to come to the aid of another. Consequently, expert swimmers may sit on the dock and watch a person drown; physicians are not required to respond to the call of a stranger who is dying; travelers are not obligated to stop at the scene of a traffic accident to assist the victims; and members of the public are not required to donate vital organs for a lifesaving transplant or to give blood for a lifesaving transfusion. Such decisions are only subject to the personal consciences of the individuals involved.

The general rule of providing no legal remedies for nonfeasance gradually eroded for those in "public callings." The first such public calling referred to innkeepers who had an affirmative duty to protect their guests, or public carriers who had a duty to protect their passengers. An innkeeper could not passively permit dangerous conditions to exist in a guest's room without warning the guest beforehand or removing the threat. Similarly, a public carrier had to take reasonable steps to insure that passengers were safely transported. The rule for nonfeasance was later expanded to include any situation where a "special relationship" existed.

Paragraph 315 of the *Restatement of Torts* expresses this rule:

> There is no duty to control the conduct of a third person as to prevent him from causing physical harm to another unless: (a) a special relation exists between the actor and the third person which imposes a duty upon the actor to control the third person's conduct. (American Law Institute, 1966, p. 857)

The key phrase is "special relation." Courts have held that a special relationship exists when a person voluntarily agrees to assume responsibility for another person. Consequently, jailers are responsible for the conduct of their prisoners and parents for the conduct of their children. The responsibility here is not absolute. Rather, the custodians are expected to use reasonable care. There is no liability when the custodians use reasonable care, or when the custodians do not know, nor have any reason to know, that more precautions are needed.

The definition of the special relationship is one of the major features of the *Tarasoff* debate. The concept of special relationship has been applied to physicians and hospitals in a number of contexts. Psychiatric hospitals have a duty to use reasonable care when they release psychiatric patients into the community and to prevent the escape of dangerous patients (see, e.g., *Fair v. United States*, 1956; *Underwood v. United States*, 1966). In addition, physicians have a responsibility to warn patients if their medications could interfere with their ability to operate machinery or drive an automobile (*Kaiser v. Suburban Transportation System*, 1965). Doctors are liable if they negligently fail to diagnose contagious diseases (*Hofmann v. Blackmon*, 1970), or if they diagnose the disease but negligently fail to warn members of the patient's family (*Skillings v. Allen*, 1919; *Wojcik v. Aluminum Company of America*, 1959).

According to *Tarasoff*, Dr. Moore, the psychotherapist, had a "special relationship" with Prosenjit Poddar. This special relationship created the obligation to act to protect an identifiable victim from Poddar's predicted behavior.

Generally speaking a professional relationship only occurs if there is a "meeting of the minds" or an agreement on the part of the health care professional to treat a patient. Patients cannot demand services from health care professionals simply by walking into their offices. Instead, the professional has to agree to undertake the treatment of the patient. The one exception applies to hospital emergency rooms. According to the federal Emergency Medical Treatment and Active Labor Act, hospitals must treat all patients in emergencies or at least stabilize their condition before transferring them to another hospital.

LIVING WITH TARASOFF

The *Tarasoff* decision angered and confused many mental health professionals. Some of the confusion was due to a misunderstanding or misinterpretation of the court's decision. Some of the anger and confusion, however, was a reaction to an apparent legal intrusion into clinical practice that created more questions than it answered. Although no statutory law or court decision can predict all the circumstances that will apply in future cases, the *Tarasoff* decision seemed to leave several questions unanswered. For example, the decision caused psychotherapists to ask what would constitute appropriate steps to discharge the duty to protect, and what are "standards of their profession" in determining when a patient is dangerous. Furthermore, the *Tarasoff* case was binding only in California, and practitioners in other states could not predict whether courts in their states would follow *Tarasoff* reasoning.

Tarasoff is only one of many decisions regarding the liability of psychotherapists who are treating dangerous patients. Like similar cases, it tries to balance public safety with patient privacy and raises questions of social utility. Does this rule, as Justice Clark stated, vitiate the effectiveness of psychotherapy and increase the danger to society?

While legal scholars and researchers debate these issues, psychotherapists must make decisions concerning the treatment of their potentially dangerous patients. Fortunately, psychotherapists need not treat their patients in a legal vacuum. Subsequent cases (and for some states, subsequent legislation) have clarified some of the questions raised by *Tarasoff*. Clinical research and experience provide guidelines for dealing with dangerous patients that fulfill legal responsibilities as well as obligations to patients and community. We cannot answer all questions, but we can narrow their scope considerably. Although the *Tarasoff* decision has problems and shortcomings, it is a decision with which therapists can live. Furthermore, with minor modifications, it may be considered a good decision.

SUBSEQUENT CASES ADDRESS
UNANSWERED OPINIONS

Since 1976 numerous courts have dealt with the issues raised by *Tarasoff* such as how to determine who is a reasonably foreseeable victim, and how to determine when danger becomes imminent. Also courts have addressed the liability issues of admitting, supervising, and discharging patients from hospitals, including those who are involuntarily hospitalized. Some details of the cases are presented so that readers can better appreciate the kinds of situations that may arise.

Identifying Reasonably Foreseeable Victims. Several courts have applied the duty to protect to those who are reasonably close to the intended victim or close to a reasonably foreseeable class of victims. In *Hedlund v. Superior Court of Orange County* (1983), LaNita Wilson brought action against psychotherapists, whom she alleged failed to warn her that one of their patients, Stephen Wilson, was of imminent danger to her. LaNita and Stephen were lovers, but they were never married. (Their identical last name is a coincidence.) Stephen had told a psychotherapist of his intention to seriously harm LaNita. Subsequently, Stephen shot and wounded LaNita and emotionally traumatized her infant son, who was with her at the time of the shooting.

13

The court concluded that the defendants had actual knowledge of Stephen's dangerousness and should have warned LaNita. Furthermore, the court agreed that the duty to protect should have extended to the infant child. The court stated:

> Nor is it unreasonable to recognize the existence of a duty to persons in close relationship to the object of a patient's threat, for the therapist must consider the existence of such persons both in evaluating the seriousness of the danger posed by the patient and in determining the appropriate steps to be taken to protect the named victim. (p. 47)

In *Peck v. The Counseling Service of Addison County* (1985) there was reason to believe that persons might be at risk, even though they were not specifically threatened. Here an outpatient told his counselor at a mental health clinic that he might burn down his parents' barn as an act of revenge against his father. In the session, however, the patient was dissuaded from such a course and promised not to carry out his threat. The counselor believed the patient and did not disclose the threats to any other staff members or to the patient's parents. Nevertheless, the patient burned the barn the next night.

The court found the counselor and her agency negligent. In this case, the patient had identified a "victim" (the barn) but the case raised the question of whether property damage fell within the purview of a duty to protect. However, arson is a special type of property damage and the burning of an identifiable barn might have placed the owners' safety at risk.

In *Schlegel v. New Milford Hospital* (2000), a Connecticut court ruled that the duty applied to an identifiable class of victims. Here a patient murdered his mother less than 24 hours after being released from a hospital. The hospital had failed to warn the mother of his dangerousness. The day before, when he was admitted to the hospital, he had struggled with the ambulance attendants who took him to the hospital, kicked and bit the attendants who tried to care for him, and bit the attending physician. Although he had not specifically threatened to kill his mother, the court noted that the patient had a background of violence toward an identifiable class of persons: those who had tried to care for him.

A final case determined that the patients of a pedophile psychiatrist belonged to an identifiable class of victims. A child psychiatrist told his supervising analyst during the course of therapy about his pedophilic interests. He offered no remorse, and, in fact, was precise about his desires. According to court documents, the treating analyst claimed that the patient/psychiatrist was revealing only a mind-set and not a pattern of action. Consequently, the supervising analyst warned his patient/psychiatrist about the limits of confidentiality if any individual were threatened and restricted his analysis to stress management. He took no action to warn or notify anyone about his patient's/psychiatrist's statements. Four months later the child psychiatrist was charged with molesting three boys (Bruni, 1998).

In addition to the issues of whether the analyst was primarily an educator or a psychotherapist and whether pedophilia falls under the category of "substantial physical harm" which invokes a duty to protect, the relevant issue was whether the patients of the psychiatrist constituted a readily identifiable class of victims.

The jury held that the supervising psychiatrist failed to use appropriate judgment in evaluating the likelihood that the analyst would molest children in the future and that a reasonable psychiatrist should have known that his patient posed a possible threat to his children/patients.

As can be seen from these cases, much of the decision concerning who is in a "close relationship" or who is part of a "reasonably foreseeable class of victims" requires judgment on the part of the psychotherapist. We see that courts have included the infant child of the victim, the owners of a barn that was burned, the mother/caretaker of a patient, and the children/patients of a pedophilic psychiatrist among those who fall into the category of an identifiable class of foreseeable victims (Analyst Found Culpable, 1998).

Determining Imminent Dangerousness. *Tarasoff* used the standard of imminent danger to others. This standard was upheld in *Jenks v. Brown* (1996) where a Michigan court dismissed the case against a psychiatrist who failed to warn a third party that his patient intended to kidnap and hide his son who was in the custody of his ex-wife. Because the patient had not expressed an intent to harm the child, there was no imminent danger and the duty to warn or protect did not apply.

However, the assessment of imminent dangerousness does not necessarily require a verbal threat (*Jablonski v. United States*, 1983).

Jablonski murdered his live-in girlfriend, Melinda Kimball. Prior to the murder, Jablonski had attempted to rape Kimball's mother. The mother reported this event to the police, who referred Jablonski to a Veterans' Administration hospital and warned a VA psychiatrist about his potential violence. The psychiatrist failed to record or pass on this warning.

Jablonski refused to stay in the hospital, but he did attend several outpatient sessions, accompanied by Kimball. She told several psychotherapists that she was afraid of Jablonski and each of them advised her to leave him. She followed their advice and left him, but Jablonski murdered her when she returned to their apartment.

The court found the psychiatrists negligent for failure to record and pass along the warning from the police, for failure to secure prior treatment records, and for failure to warn the victim. While the psychiatrists had advised Kimball to move away from Jablonski, the court concluded: "The warnings . . . were totally unspecific and inadequate under the circumstances" (p. 398). In addition, the court held that psychotherapists could be held liable even when they did not have actual knowledge of dangerousness because they "should have known."

The court adopted a sound principle in this case: Under certain circumstances, a reasonably prudent psychotherapist may predict dangerousness even without a specific verbal threat. In this case, however, the court did not appear to apply that principle appropriately. It seems unreasonable that the court found the psychiatrists' advice to Kimball to leave Jablonski to be "nonspecific and inadequate."

Sometimes the determination of a duty hinges on the term "imminent." In a Georgia case, a psychologist warned members of the police department of threats against them by a disgruntled police officer. The psychologist noted that he considered the threats to be serious, although the danger was not imminent. He had delayed 2 weeks between learning of the threat and issuing the warning. A court found him guilty of negligence (Jury Faults Ga. Psychologist, 2000).

However, a Louisiana court interpreted the standard of dangerousness broadly. A patient made a serious and credible threat to harm a judge who had overturned a verdict in his favor. The patient claimed that he knew where the judge lived, when and where she jogged, where she parked her car, and that he had looked into her windows at night. In addition, he carried a gun. Both the treating psychiatrist and psychologist warned the judge which led to the eventual arrest of the patient.

After being arrested, the patient was committed involuntarily to a psychiatric hospital. The patient sued, alleging that the psychiatrist should have committed him involuntarily at the outset, rather than first warning the judge. He also alleged that the warning was unnecessary because the threat, although serious and credible, was not imminent. The trial jury and subsequent appeals court exonerated the psychiatrist and psychologist from any wrongdoing (*Viviano v. Moan*, 1994).

The determination of the dangerousness of a threat depends, to a large extent, on the circumstances and it is not possible to list all of the factors that would make one threat imminent and another not imminent. However, it should be noted that in the Louisiana case, the patient had taken actions in furtherance of his threat (found where the judge lived, monitored her schedule, etc.), whereas the patient in Georgia had only discussed his fantasies of harming the potential victim.

ATTEMPTS TO EXPAND TARASOFF

Some plaintiffs have attempted to expand the *Tarasoff* decision to apply to situations when the danger was not reasonably foreseeable. For example, in *Matter of Estate of Votteler* (1982), the court refused to find liability when the patient's husband withheld information about her violent behavior from the doctor. Lola, a patient of Dr. Votteler, had seriously injured a woman by driving an automobile over her. The injured woman sued Dr. Votteler because, she claimed, he should have warned his patient's husband about her violent nature and that the husband could have warned her. Although Lola had a background of violence, especially toward her husband, her husband withheld a lot of information about her violent behavior from Dr. Votteler. At the trial, the husband testified that he "did not tell the doctor about Lola's violence because he wasn't specifically asked about her behavior" (p. 761). The assaulted woman also knew about Lola's violent and threatening behavior but "she contends that she would have taken the situation seriously only if a warning originated with a professional like Dr. Votteler" (p. 761). The court rejected the *Tarasoff* claim. The doctor was not required to issue a warning because the plaintiff already had more knowledge about the danger than the doctor.

Plaintiffs have also tried to extend *Tarasoff* so that the psychotherapists could be liable to the assailants/patients. For example, in *Cole v. Taylor* (1981), a former patient sued her psychiatrist on the grounds that he failed to prevent her from murdering her former husband. Later, the patient sued her psychiatrist for negligence because he failed to stop her from murdering her ex-husband. She also invoked the *Tarasoff* decision, because, she claimed, the psychiatrist failed to warn her ex-husband of the danger to him.

Her claim was quickly rejected. The court stated that the *Tarasoff* decision was inapplicable because it only dealt with the duty to the intended victim and not to the assailant. Furthermore, the court noted that "as a general rule [a] person cannot maintain action if . . . he must rely in whole or in part, on [an] illegal or immoral act or transaction to which he is a party" (p. 766). The court did not elaborate on the social harm which would be done if murderers could act willfully and then project responsibility for their acts upon psychotherapists.

Attempts to expand *Tarasoff* will fail in those situations in which state legislatures have delineated the responsibilities of psychotherapists in a statute or regulation. For example, in *Thapar v. Zezulka* (1999), the Texas Supreme Court refused to find a psychiatrist liable for failing to warn an identifiable third party of the threats against his life. The court pointed to the Texas statute that permitted, but did not require, psychotherapists to warn law enforcement officials if patients presented a danger to themselves or others.

The rule in facilities governed by federal drug and alcohol laws is unclear. There is no exception to the federal confidentiality law in situations where a patient presents an imminent threat to harm a third party. It would appear that no warning can be given. However, there is the possibility that a warning can be given without identifying that the source is a treatment center for alcohol or other drugs.

Finally, we were unable to find any cases where the *Tarasoff* decision was expanded to include a duty to report past crimes. The general rule is that psychotherapists are not obligated to, or even permitted, to report past crimes of their patients. Although the privileged communication or confidentiality statutes may vary somewhat from state to state or within the same state from profession to profession, the general rule is that information obtained in psychotherapy is confidential and may not be released without the consent of the patient, without a court order, or as explicitly permitted by a statute.

An unusual twist occurred in *Illinois v. Ranstrom* (1999) in which a patient reported to his psychotherapist that he had attacked his ex-girlfriend's current boyfriend. After the patient terminated treatment, the psychotherapist notified the police and the evidence given was used to convict the former patient. In an appeal of the verdict, the court refused to exclude the evidence of the psychotherapist because the psychotherapist gave the information in order to protect the third party from imminent danger of harm. This case involved the use of information obtained in the warning. However, if the former patient had not presented an imminent danger to third parties, the psychotherapist would not have been able to disclose the information about the past crime. Furthermore, individual judges interpreting laws in different states may reach different conclusions. A New York court ruled that a previous warning did not constitute a waiver of the psychotherapist-patient privilege (*Tarasoff* Warning Does Not Waive Psychotherapy Privilege, 2000).

SPECIAL ISSUES WITH HOSPITALIZED PATIENTS

As noted earlier, *Tarasoff* was based in part on case law dealing with the negligent release of patients from psychiatric hospitals. The case law on negligent release has changed little since *Tarasoff*.

Hospitals are liable for negligence in releasing or for granting leaves to patients, or for failing to prevent the escape of involuntarily committed patients. For example, in *Bradley Center v. Wessner* (1982), a man had admitted himself voluntarily to Bradley Center for depression and anger toward his wife for having an affair with another man. The woman had made known her intent to divorce her husband. During the weekend of February 7 and 8, 1975, Wessner had been given a pass to visit his children. During that time he secured a gun, confronted his wife and her paramour, and shot them both. The court held that the "criminal act was reasonably foreseeable . . . and that the death of their mother [Mrs. Wessner] was proximately caused by appellant's negligence" (p. 719). The crucial piece of evidence in this case was the nurse's notes of February 5th and 6th that recorded Mr. Wessner's threats against his wife. "He made a statement that he had a weapon and was just waiting for the right circumstances" (p. 719). Although the wife knew of the threats, the facility had the power to refuse the leave request because state law allowed it to detain voluntary patients for 48 hours before a release was mandated.

The *Bradley Center* case dealt with the failure to detain a voluntary patient. Special liability issues emerge when treating involuntary patients. The procedures and criteria for involuntary hospitalizations vary across the states and provinces, although they typically specify that the person must be severely mentally ill and present a danger to self or others, often through an overt act. Other clinical data such as violent thoughts, fantasies, or verbal threats may provide clinical support for the commitment decision, but they may not be sufficient in and of themselves, from a legal point of view, to justify a commitment.

Most courts hold that the prerequisites of a malpractice suit do not exist when the admitting physician or psychologist only examines a prospective patient for a civil commitment. However, a malpractice suit could occur if the commitment was initiated against a person with whom a treatment relationship had already existed. Also, for malpractice principles to apply, the psychotherapist's treatment must fall below an acceptable standard of care, the patient must have been harmed, and the harm must have been caused by the therapist's inadequate or inappropriate treatment.

Furthermore, psychotherapists could face other tort damages based upon other legal remedies such as malicious prosecution, false imprisonment, abuse of process, or for deprivation of civil liberties under the Civil Rights Act of 1872. Each of these legal remedies has certain prerequisites (Knapp & VandeCreek, 1987). For a charge of malicious prosecution to have standing, the commitment proceeding must have terminated in favor of the plaintiff, harmed the plaintiff, lacked probable cause, and must have been initiated with "malice" and not justice as a motive. False imprisonment refers to an illegal confinement within a restricted area such as a hospital by force or threat of force. Abuse of process occurs when legal proceedings are used to accomplish purposes for which they were not designed (Prosser & Keaton, 1985). For abuse of process to apply, a civil commitment would have to have been initiated for reasons other than treatment of mental illness or protection of society, such as to aid a family in ridding itself of an unwanted or troublesome member.

Generally speaking, patients resent the use of force that is used or implied in the involuntary hospitalization procedures. The best risk management strategy for psychotherapists is to ensure that they follow the letter and spirit of the civil commitment laws before such a step is taken.

Fortunately, many states have "good faith" immunities for actions taken in conjunction with involuntary hospitalization procedures. As long as the psychotherapists follow the law and document their actions with a reasonable degree of documentation, such suits are likely to fail.

For example, in *Doby v. DeCrescenzo* (1999), a federal court refused to uphold a civil rights action against a psychiatrist who admitted a woman to the hospital after she had threatened suicide. Even though the evaluation of the psychiatrist may have failed to meet acceptable standards of professional conduct (he allegedly failed to ask her about her depressive symptoms, adequately evaluate her suicidality, or consider less restrictive means of treatment), it did not meet the standard of gross negligence as required in Pennsylvania's civil commitment law.

In contrast to the negligent commitment of patients, there may also be liability for the failure to commit or to take reasonable steps to implement a commitment. For example, in *Greenberg v. Barbour* (1971), a physician had referred a patient for a civil commitment but failed to mention the life-endangering qualities of his behavior. The patient was not committed and subsequently assaulted a third party. The court held that the accepted standards of treatment involved conveying the life-endangering facts concerning the patient when seeking a commitment.

Generally psychotherapists and hospitals are not liable for court-ordered patient releases. For example, the case of *Teasley v. United States* (1980) involved a woman who was attacked by a former mental patient. The victim sued the hospital for releasing the patient. The suit failed because the hospital staff had requested an involuntary commitment of the patient but the court had rejected the request. This case differs from *Hicks v. United States* (1975), in which a plaintiff successfully sued hospital employees even though the patient had been released by the court. In *Hicks*, the hospital staff had negligently failed to provide the court with full and accurate details of the patient's mental condition. In *Teasley*, the hospital staff correctly informed the court of the patient's dangerous qualities and told the court that he would be a danger to society if released.

IMMUNITY PROVISIONS

Generally, government officials who create statutes and regulations, and administrators of facilities who must exercise their judgment in implementing the regulations, are immune from liability. However, psychotherapists and others who actually provide the hands-on patient care are liable for failure to exercise due care. Courts often make the distinction about which officials are immune from liability by examining whether the actions or judgments were "discretionary" or "ministerial."

Discretionary functions refer to judgment calls about how to implement regulations. Examples would be decisions as to whether regulations permit the institution to grant a leave from a hospital for a patient to visit family or friends, or whether an open-door policy for suicidal patients is an acceptable treatment approach. Ministerial functions, in contrast, refer to actions taken with specific patients by psychotherapists or other personnel who are in direct contact with the patient. With this distinction, a hospital administrator may be immune from liability for implementing treatment programs permitted by state law, but in the same case a psychotherapist could be liable for negligence in carrying out the treatment plan.

Immunity laws provide a patchwork of exceptions that vary considerably among the states. The wording of immunity laws is important in determining the scope of possible liability. Some immunity statutes provide protection only for decisions made in good faith. Unreasonable acts or releases made in bad faith would not qualify under such a statute. Other statutes specify that the immunity only applies to the government and not to its employees.

CLINICAL RECOMMENDATIONS
WHEN PATIENTS THREATEN OTHERS

Appelbaum (1985) stated that the responsibilities under *Tarasoff* can be met best by following a three-step process: assessing dangerousness thoroughly, formulating the optimal treatment plan, and implementing the treatment plan. Liability may occur because of faulty judgment or behavior during any of these stages.

Assessment of Dangerousness. The assessment of dangerousness is an ongoing process, not a one-time event. From the first session in which the patient gives indications of intent to harm another person, until the last session of therapy, the psychotherapist should inquire about and keep alert for signs that violence may occur.

Although no box score or formula can predict dangerousness with any degree of accuracy, research and clinical information can guide psychotherapists in their decision making. Otto (2000) noted that the different methods used by psychotherapists for determining the risk of violence rest on a continuum of structure starting with unstructured clinical interviews to structured interviews to highly structured actuarial tables. Although each method has its strengths and limitations, Otto recommends a combined approach whereby psychotherapists rely in part on clinical information, guided or directed interviews, actuarial tables, and other methods to reach their conclusion.

Dangerousness prediction scales have been developed for various population groups (Dangerous Behavior Rating Scale [Menzies, Webster, & Sepejak, 1985]; Violence Risk Appraisal Guide [Harris & Quincy, 1993]; Hare Psychopathology Checklist Revised [Hare, 1991]; and the MacArthur Scales [Monahan et al., 2000]). These scales typically rely on static items that cannot be changed (sex, early childhood history, etc.) and dynamic factors (current psychopathology, violent fantasies, etc.) that can change. However, their application to populations other than those upon whom they were standardized is uncertain. For example, the MacArthur Violence Risk Assessment Scale, which was developed from a prospective study of violent behavior in persons discharged from psychiatric hospitals in three different cities, may not generalize to patients seen as psychiatric outpatients or in prisons.

Nonetheless, one scale of particular usefulness may be the HCR-20 (Douglas et al., 1999; Webster et al., 1997; see Table 1, p. 24). The "H" refers to 10 historical items, the "C" refers to 5 clinical items, and the "R" refers to 5 risk management items. It has good predictive validity with patients who were involuntarily hospitalized, but should be used cautiously with other populations.

In addition to the use of the scale, the clinician can ask the patient for detailed information about any violent episodes in the past. Some of the questions could include: "What kind of harm occurred?" "Who were the victims?" "What caused the violence?" "What was the context of the violence?" and "Are there patterns to these violent episodes?" (Otto, 2000). It may also be useful to ask patients: "How do you feel about the violence?" "What did you learn from the situation?" "How would you have handled the situation differently?" and "How would you try to avoid the violence in similar situations in the future?" Psychotherapists

---

TABLE 1: HCR-20 ITEMS*

A. *Historical Items*

    1. Previous violence
    2. Young age at first violent incident
    3. Relationship instability
    4. Employment problems
    5. Substance use problems
    6. Major mental illness
    7. Psychopathy
    8. Early maladjustment
    9. Personality disorder
   10. Prior supervision failure

B. *Clinical Items*

    1. Lack of insight [into mental disorder]
    2. Negative attitudes [toward others, institutions, social agencies, the law]
    3. Active symptoms of major mental illness
    4. Impulsivity
    5. Unresponsive to treatment

C. *Risk Management Items*

    1. Plans lack feasibility
    2. Exposure to destabilizers [weapons, substances, potential victims]
    3. Lack of personal support
    4. Noncompliance with remediation attempts
    5. Stress

---

should be especially alert to any role that alcohol or other drugs may have played in these events.

Finally, psychotherapists need to consider the overall life situation and psychological state of the patient. Some of the factors to look for are verbal threats to harm others, accessibility of weapons, relationship to intended victim(s), abuse of alcohol or other drugs, presence of paranoia or sociopathy, membership in a social group that condones or encourages violence, and therapeutic relationship variables such as the degree of adherence and commitment to treatment, and the strength of the therapeutic alliance (Beauford, McNiel, & Binder, 1997; Lidz, Mulvey, & Gardner, 1993; Monahan, 1993; Swartz et al., 1998; Truscott, Evans, & Mansell, 1995). The importance of interviewing significant others becomes more salient when it is considered that more than half of the targeted victims of violence are family members other than a child (McNiel, Binder, & Fulton, 1998; Tardiff & Koenigsberg, 1985).

Stalking or the willful and malicious following of another person presents its own unique features. The assessment and management of stalkers requires knowledge of their unique pathology (Meloy, 1997).

In addition, homicidal persons have an increased risk of suicidal behavior and vice versa. Psychotherapists should routinely ask homicidal persons about their thoughts of suicide and routinely ask suicidal persons about their thoughts of harming others.

Even after gathering an extensive amount of information on the patient, however, predictions of future violence cannot be made with complete accuracy. Indeed, Monahan and Steadman (1996) have compared the prediction of violent behavior by psychotherapists to the prediction of the weather by meteorologists. Both types of predictions are often inaccurate. Nonetheless, the courts will hold psychotherapists to the standards of what reasonable psychotherapists would have done in assessing violence.

Two areas of assessment warrant special comment: assessment of possible partner abuse and assessment of dangerous children.

Assessment of Domestic Abuse. Spousal abuse may be the most common type of violence encountered by psychotherapists. Clues for dangerousness include threats of homicide or a history of violence against the partner, emotional abuse (persistent and severe insults or cursing), or a history of pet abuse. Because many partners may be reluctant to admit that they perpetrate (or are victims of) violence, it may be prudent to start questioning about domestic abuse indirectly. Some of the first questions might be: "How do you resolve your disagreements?" "What was the worst disagreement that you ever had?" and "Have you ever felt afraid?"

Also, some patients have restrictive definitions of what constitutes abuse (Otto, 2000). Consequently, it may be necessary to ask patients whether they were ever pushed, shoved, slapped, grabbed, had their movements restricted, or had objects thrown at them.

Furthermore, women who leave their abusive partners are at an increased risk for being victimized by serious violence (Riggs, Caufield, & Street, 2000). A psychotherapist may need to warn the intended victim even if the victim has already been threatened directly. For example, in *Emerich v. Philadelphia Center for Human Development*

(1998), a psychotherapist warned a girlfriend that her partner had threatened to kill her if she attempted to move her belongings out of their apartment. She ignored the warning and was subsequently killed. The executors of her estate sued, alleging that the warning was not adequate. The court disagreed, however, and exonerated the psychotherapist from any liability.

Assessment of Dangerous Children. The general principles for assessing dangerousness among adults apply to assessing dangerousness among children. Again, no simple box score can predict who will or will not act violently. Instead, the assessment requires a determination of the clinical features of the patient and a detailed review of any past acts of violence on the child's part. One difference is that there is not yet a predictive scale for youth violence that can be useful across a variety of clinical settings (Borum, 2000). Another difference in the assessment of violence among children is that collateral sources, such as parents, siblings, school, or other social agencies, may be more available and relied upon for more information than is typically found in the assessment of violence among adults.

Formulating the Treatment Plan. The second step is to develop a reasonable treatment plan designed to reduce the likelihood of danger. If psychotherapists determine that a patient represents a danger to an identifiable person or class of persons, then they are obligated to try to diffuse the danger. As noted previously, the *Tarasoff* doctrine does not require warning the intended victim as the only therapeutic response when danger arises. Instead, the court stated that the "discharge of such duty may require the therapist to take one or more of various steps, depending on the nature of the case, including warning the intended victim" (p. 334). According to *Tarasoff*, the treating psychotherapist may attempt an involuntary commitment, notify the police, or take other steps to deter the violence.

Of course, as noted earlier, some state statutes specify certain activities, such as warning the intended victim or seeking an involuntary hospitalization, as the appropriate way to respond when a patient threatens to harm an identifiable third person. Even in states that allow a full range of therapeutic interventions to diffuse the violent situation, the difficulties in determining the treatment plan remain significant because no data can guide the psychotherapist as to the optimal intervention.

For example, no evidence suggests that warning the intended victim is more effective than handling the situation through a hospitalization, referral for medication, or traditional therapy. Instead, psychotherapists are left to their clinical judgment, consistent with the standards of care or judgment of average and reasonable psychotherapists, as to what the optimal intervention would be. Although warning the intended victim may make sense in some situations, in other situations the warning might actually precipitate the violence that the psychotherapist is trying to prevent.

Although statutes or common sense may state that informing a police department is an acceptable way to discharge duties engendered by *Tarasoff*, a survey of police departments in Michigan and South Carolina showed that many police departments do not have experience with *Tarasoff*-type warnings or even have policies governing their actions if they receive such a warning (Huber et al., 2000). Consequently, the decision to notify the police may or may not be adequate depending on the response of the police department or knowledge of how they have responded to similar calls in the past.

The decisions about the treatment plan can focus on incapacitating the patient (such as through a hospitalization), hardening the target (such as through warning the intended victim), or by intensifying treatment (Monahan, 1993). In states that have adopted *Tarasoff*, the psychologist can choose among the three options depending on which is most likely to protect the public in the long run. In states that have "duty to protect" statutes that specify warning the intended victim as a method of avoiding liability for the actions of their patients, the option of intensifying treatment cannot exonerate the psychotherapist from liability in the event that a tragedy were to occur. The states that prohibit warning the identified victim limit the psychotherapists to either incapacitating the patient or intensifying treatment.

At times, it may be necessary to place patients in seclusion or in restraints. Taking such steps raises additional ethical and legal issues.

Seclusions and Restraints. As noted previously, the decision to protect a third party or to make an exception to the general rule of confidentiality requires an exception to the general moral principle of fidelity to the psychotherapist-patient relationship and respect for patient autonomy. Although the exception may be justified, it is necessary to minimize the intrusion to fidelity and respect for patient autonomy as much as possible.

At times, hospitals may need to restrain aggressive patients or place them in seclusion to protect other patients. When this happens, it is desirable to minimize the intrusion upon the patient's autonomy as much as possible. Every effort should be made to anticipate the circumstances that could give rise to violence and to use nonviolent means to diffuse situations when the threat of violence does arise.

In response to reports of patient deaths from seclusions or restraints, the Health Care Financing Administration (HCFA) has established standards for seclusions and restraints that apply to hospitals that participate in Medicare or Medicaid programs (Clarke, 2000). These rules prohibit hospitals from using restraints or seclusions as a means of discipline, coercion, convenience, or retaliation. Every patient in restraint or seclusion must have a face-to-face evaluation by a physician or other independent practitioner every hour (Medicare and Medicaid Programs, 1999). In addition, states may have standards that go beyond those imposed by HCFA. Conscientious hospitals will know the statutes and regulations that apply in their state, train their staff in their proper use, and make concerted efforts to reduce the number of restraint and seclusion orders.

Implementing the Treatment Plan. The intervention must be implemented in a reasonable manner. Inadequately implemented interventions have led to tragedies. Even in *Tarasoff*, liability occurred because the psychologist had failed to implement the intervention as intended. The treating psychologist correctly identified the patient as dangerous and had initiated an involuntary commitment reasonably calculated to diffuse the danger. The murder occurred, however, when the police failed to follow through with the commitment and the supervisor of the psychologist ordered him to take no further actions to protect Ms. Tarasoff.

When it is necessary to warn a potential victim, it is best to try to implement the treatment plan with the consent or participation of the patient. Although not always possible, the warning might be made with the patient present or at least with the consent of the patient. Binder and McNiel (1996) found that patients who participated in the decision to warn were less likely to discontinue psychotherapy. When patients were informed of the need or intention to protect an identifiable third party, they were more likely to continue in treatment, although a few did express anger at the warning being made.

Binder and McNiel (1996) also found that in most situations in which a warning was made, the intended victims already knew of the danger to them. The most common response by the potential victims was appreciation and an expressed intent to modify their behavior. Some intended victims, however, responded with a denial of the danger. In those situations, it may be advisable to send the intended victim a certified letter reiterating the danger. The letter could help reinforce the psychologist's verbal warning about the danger involved. In addition, this paper trail will document the effort of the psychologist to protect the intended victim.

If a hospitalization is being considered, then it is best to involve the patient in the decision, if at all possible. It may mean persuasion ("It is for your benefit to enter the hospital because. . . .") or inducements ("If you enter the hospital voluntarily you will retain the option of signing yourself out. . . ."). Threats ("If you do not enter the hospital voluntarily, then it will be necessary to initiate an involuntary hospitalization. . . .") should be avoided, although in some situations they may be necessary.

If the decision is made to hospitalize the patient, then the psychotherapist should be certain that the hospital (especially the attending physician) understands the danger involved. The dissemination of accurate information is especially problematic whenever there are multiple treatment providers such as in a hospital or nonhospital residential facility. The emergency room or admitting personnel may not convey the severity of the dangerousness to the treating professionals.

As can be readily inferred, Appelbaum's three stages of decision making can overlap considerably. The assessment of dangerousness needs to be made periodically throughout the treatment process and the treatment plan may have to be modified as the clinical realities and external circumstances of the patient change.

For example, treatment plans may need to be modified if the patient is noncompliant with the original treatment plan. A program of intensive outpatient treatment may be sufficient to fulfill the duty to protect at one point in the therapeutic process, but the failure of the patient to comply with that treatment plan may necessitate a revision of the strategies designed to diffuse the threat of violence.

PATIENT SUICIDES

Recent large-scale epidemiological studies have shown that the rate of suicide has increased substantially over the last 50 years. Young persons in the United States have a rate of suicide that is 10 times higher than that of their grandparents. Suicide is one of the leading causes of death among American teenagers. Not only is depression much more common, but major depression episodes are occurring earlier for young Americans (Seligman, 1989).

A patient's suicide is bound to jar the confidence of even the most competent psychotherapist. He or she may spend many hours second-guessing the treatment plan and wondering what could have been done differently. The reactions of the family members of the patients may vary considerably. Some relatives readily acknowledge the efforts of psychotherapists and thank them for their efforts. Others may display extreme and irrational hostility.

As with threats to third parties, threats of suicide involve both ethical and legal issues. Any intervention requires a consideration of the ethical principles of beneficence (acting to protect the patient), nonmaleficence (avoiding doing anything that would harm the patient), and respect for patient autonomy. As much as possible it is desirable for the psychotherapist to respect patient autonomy and to intrude upon the patient's wishes only where it is necessary to protect the safety of the patient. If it is necessary for beneficence to "trump" respect for patient autonomy, then every effort should be made to do so in a compassionate and respectful manner.

In addition to the ethical issues and any personal anguish involved, psychotherapists also face legal issues when patients threaten suicide. Patient suicides are one of the most frequent causes of malpractice suits. The standards for malpractice in the case of a patient suicide are the same as the standards for other malpractice cases. That is, the court will evaluate whether the care of the patient fell below the minimum level expected of a prudent and reasonable psychologist. Generally, courts will not find therapists liable when the suicide attempt was not reasonably foreseeable. Therefore, no liability has been found when cooperative and apparently contented patients suddenly attempted suicide (*Carlino v. State*, 1968; *Dalton v. State*, 1970), or when an aggressive patient failed to reveal suicidal intent (*Paradies v. Benedictine Hospi-*

tal, 1980). In contrast, courts have held practitioners or hospitals culpable when the treatment plan overlooked or neglected evidence of suicidal tendencies (*Dinnerstein v. United States*, 1973).

In evaluating liability, courts also usually assess the reasonableness of professional judgment in the treatment of a suicidal patient. The failure to take reasonable precautions when suicidal intent is obvious would be grounds for liability. Nevertheless, practitioners must only demonstrate that reasonable precautions were taken.

Finally, courts will evaluate the thoroughness with which the treatment plan was implemented. Thus, in *Comiskey v. State of New York* (1979), a hospital (but not the physician) was found liable for failure to implement the physician's instructions to closely observe a suicidal patient. In contrast, the failure of a psychotherapist to inform other staff members about the suicidal potential of a patient would leave the psychotherapist at fault but absolve the uninformed staff (Perr, 1985).

INPATIENT SUICIDES

Plaintiffs can present legal actions against the hospital and/or the psychotherapists for inpatient suicides. The plaintiffs generally will sue the physicians or psychotherapists within the hospital if they have staff or hospital privileges. Although these professionals may use the hospital facilities, they are assumed to be independent and responsible for their professional judgments.

However, the plaintiff could also sue the hospital if it negligently hired or trained its employees, supervised them inadequately, or tolerated hazardous facilities. In addition, if the hospital employed the physicians or psychotherapists, then it could be sued for the negligent actions of the staff members under the doctrine of vicarious liability. The negligent employees, however, may not be entirely free from liability because the hospital could, in turn, sue them for the financial loss incurred by their actions (King, 1977).

In considering malpractice actions for inpatient suicides, the courts have slowly but steadily changed the standards of liability from an earlier "custodial model" to a more recent "open-door" model. According to the custodial model, patients were hospitalized to diagnose suicidal intent and then to protect them from their self-destructive impulses through close supervision. The strict standard of supervision turned psychotherapists into jailers with white coats.

Mary McCarthy described the strict custodial model in her novel, *The Group* (1964). Kay was committed involuntarily to Payne Whitney Clinic by her husband. One day, when she received a visit from her friend Polly, Kay exclaimed:

"Heavens, I'm glad you're here! You don't know the terrible things they've been doing to me, Polly." Last night the nurses had taken her belt away from her. "I can't wear my dress without a belt." They had taken her nightgown sash too ("Look!") and they tried to take her wedding ring, but she would not let them. "We had a frightful struggle, practically a wrestling match, but then the head nurse came and said to let me keep it for the night. . . . After that, they made me open my mouth and looked in to see if I had any removable bridges. . . ." "I gather," Kay went on in a different tone, "that they think I want to commit suicide. They keep peering at me through those slats in the door. Did they expect me to hang myself with my belt? And what was I supposed to do with my wedding ring? Swallow it." Polly's answer was prompt; she thought the nurses would have done better to explain it to Kay. (pp. 325-326)

Kay's experiences illustrate the shortcomings of the protective model. Although the suicidal precautions prevented Kay from attempting suicide, they also deprived her of basic sources of dignity and pleasure.

But even when the hospital applied the custodial model, there was no guarantee that patients could not commit suicide. Nonetheless, the courts have found liability only for reasonably foreseeable suicide attempts. In *Moore v. United States* (1963), the hospital was not found negligent when the patient pried open the detention screen from the third floor and jumped out. Although the patient had delusions and paranoid ideation, he had shown no evidence of suicidal intent. Similarly, in *Hirsch v. State* (1960), the hospital was absolved of blame when a patient committed suicide with capsules he had secreted. The hospital employees had stripped him naked and searched him. No one had reason to suspect that he had successfully concealed barbiturates.

Some of the strict precautions that were considered routine 30 years ago probably encouraged patients to remain depressed and to perceive themselves as helpless. Patients who were hospitalized for long periods of time under strict conditions often underestimated their potential for recovery and became more dependent on the hospital, family, or friends.

Current legal standards recognize that the treatment of suicidal patients may often involve some degree of risk. Although in the long run it may be better to treat the patient in the community, there are short-term risks that the patient may attempt or succeed at suicide. This philosophy was expressed in *Dinnerstein v. United States* (1973):

> [Not] every potential suicide must be locked in a padded cell. The law and modern psychiatry have now both come to the belated conclusion that an overly restrictive environment can be as destructive as a permissive one. (p. 38)

Now courts recognize that clinicians must balance the benefits of treatment against the risks of freedom. Psychologists must use reasonable professional judgment in assessing the therapeutic risks of freedom. They must carefully assess the decision to reduce the supervision of suicidal patients, whether it involves a transfer to a less restrictive ward or a discharge out of the hospital. Of course, when the patient is imminently suicidal, the hospital must still provide close supervision. "An open door policy does not mean an open window policy for highly suicidal patients" (Knapp & VandeCreek, 1983, p. 277).

OUTPATIENT SUICIDES

The movement toward outpatient treatment has increased with advances in behavioral and pharmacological treatments. Also, as civil commitment laws became more stringent, many patients could no longer be forced into hospital treatment only because they threatened suicide or needed treatment.

The principles for establishing liability for outpatient suicides are generally the same as for inpatient cases. Psychotherapists must use reasonable standards of care in the diagnosis of suicidal intent and the development and implementation of a treatment plan.

CLINICAL RECOMMENDATIONS

Appelbaum's (1985) three-step procedure for assessing therapists' responsibilities under *Tarasoff* duty-to-protect situations can also be useful for evaluating the responsibilities of psychotherapists in situations where patients threaten to harm themselves. The three steps are to assess the danger of suicide, formulate the treatment plan, and implement it. Liability may occur because of faulty judgment or behavior during any of these stages.

Assessing Risk of Self-Harm. As with the assessment of dangerousness to others, no box score or formula can be given to derive a reliable "suicidality quotient." Nonetheless, the risk of suicide can be estimated by considering current suicidal ideation, hopelessness, recurrent major depressive or bipolar disorder, substance abuse or dependence, schizophrenia, a personality disorder, or unemployment status (Brown et al., 2000). Other factors to consider are verbal threats to harm oneself, previous attempts, the presence of a plan and availability of means to do so (especially relevant are the availability of guns or lethal drugs), overall physical health, presence of a social support system or religious belief system, therapeutic relationship variables such as the degree of adherence and commitment to treatment, and the strength of the therapeutic alliance (Bongar et al., 1992). This list is not all-inclusive and other factors should be considered, depending on the specific patient or set of circumstances. For example, the stress of incarceration when coupled with other preexisting problems may make suicide a high risk for prisoners (Bonner, 1992).

Psychological testing is not a substitute for the clinical judgment of the psychotherapist. However, testing may help clarify, support, or modify initial clinical impressions.

In making their assessment of suicidal risk, psychotherapists can also consider protective factors or factors that increase the desire of the patient to live. These factors may include religious or moral beliefs against suicide, a sense of responsibility to family members, the presence of coping skills, and fear of death (Malone et al., 2000).

The courts will not hold the psychotherapist liable only because a patient committed suicide. Instead, the plaintiffs must prove that the psychotherapists were negligent in their assessment or treatment. Psychotherapists can demonstrate the adequacy of their treatment through consulting with other psychotherapists and documenting treatment decisions carefully. The importance of seeking consultation in difficult situations cannot be overestimated. Difficult patients sometimes create countertransference reactions that can impair the objectivity of the psychotherapist. Documentation should be quite explicit around treatment decisions such as the decision to hospitalize or not to hospitalize. In addition, any treatment decision to reduce suicidal watch, allow leaves, or otherwise grant more freedom should be documented carefully. Discharged patients should be given follow-up appointments because suicide rates are especially high shortly after discharge.

The manner of documentation can be as important as the documentation itself. A brief note stating, "the patient is suicidal" probably creates as much confusion as enlightenment. It is not known how the observer arrived at that conclusion, if the patient threatened suicide, or if it reflects an unsubstantiated inference on the part of the writer. Instead, notes should be more specific as to the reasons for the conclusion.

Development of the Treatment Plan. Clinicians are responsible for developing a treatment plan consistent with reasonable professional standards. The treatment plan should be developed in a manner designed to reduce suicidality and concomitant depression. Options include outpatient psychotherapy, outpatient psychotherapy combined with medication, and psychiatric hospitalization. For outpatient treatment, some of the precautions are well established: if medication is prescribed, the amount of medication distributed should be nonlethal, and psychotherapists should offer 24-hour availability if needed; frequent therapeutic contacts; and frequent evaluations of the need for hospitalizations. Deviations from these norms should be documented and the reasons why indicated. Psychotherapists who cannot provide this level of care should refer such patients.

The support and sensitive watchfulness of the family can aid recovery. If the threat to harm is imminent, psychotherapists have the option of notifying members of a support system of the patient's high risk.

At times patients may engage in cutting or other forms of self-mutilation to punish themselves, reduce emotional distress, or draw attention to themselves. Although these and other forms of self-mutilation are not always considered suicide attempts, they often coexist with serious suicidality. The treatment plan should not involve an automatic reaction to hospitalize that may, under certain circumstances, be clinically contraindicated.

For some persons who engage in nonlethal self-mutilation, hospitalization may represent a step toward regression and loss of personal responsibility. Instead, psychotherapists should carefully consider clinical interventions designed to reduce the psychological disorder and the cutting.

"No harm" contracts may help some patients. However, to be effective, these contracts must reflect the honest intent of the patient to comply. They are only as reliable as the soundness of the therapeutic alliance (Simon, 2000). A "no harm" contract signed under duress or pressure is probably of little clinical value. Furthermore, psychotherapists should not allow a "no harm" contract to lead them to be overconfident in their treatment. It is not unheard of for a patient to sign a contract, but later to become overwhelmed by suicidal thoughts and act upon them. The intent of the patients during the therapy hour when they sign the contract may not remain with them after they leave the office.

Environmental manipulations such as having guns removed from the house or having the family members keep a close eye on the suicidal patient may also be indicated.

Within hospitals, the degree of observation needs to vary according to the needs of the patient. It may be necessary to place the patient on one-on-one observation, and conduct total body searches (including body cavities). In some cases the intrusive observations may be forced on the patient unwillingly, but if they are implemented in a beneficent and respectful manner, the patient may derive some therapeutic benefit from it. Patients under observation reported that staff members who engage in pleasant and hope-engendering conversation make the observation a therapeutically beneficial experience as well as a necessary safety precaution.

A review of some actual recent cases reveals how courts interpret the duty to assess and treat suicidal patients properly. In *McNamara v. Honeyman* (1989), a hospital was found negligent when a psychiatrist took a patient off round-the-clock, one-on-one observation and instead ordered 15-minute checks. The patient had exhibited suicidal behavior up to 3 days prior to hanging herself. Expert testimony suggested that continual observation should have been maintained until the patient had shown at least 2 weeks of nonsuicidal behavior.

In *O'Sullivan v. Presbyterian Hospital* (1995), the court ruled that sufficient grounds existed for a malpractice case when a patient committed suicide a few months after seeking treatment from the outpatient department of the hospital. Although the patient had not expressed any suicidal ideation in the intake interview, the hospital failed to obtain his past treatment records or request a medical evaluation despite a serious loss of weight, had offered the patient no medication, and had twice offered the patient group therapy, only to have the patient denied entrance into the groups offered. Finally, the hospital failed to schedule an interview with the patient's sister who allegedly called the hospital several times to provide background information on her brother.

In *Darren v. Safier* (1994), however, the court held that the psychiatrist was not liable for the suicide of a patient who died 1 month after being discharged from the hospital. The patient had expressed no suicidal ideation and there was no evidence that the psychiatrist had deviated from acceptable professional standards of care even though, in hindsight, he made an error in judgment.

Implementing the Treatment Plan. The best treatment plan means little unless it is implemented as intended. Courts have found hospitals liable when the ward personnel did not follow through with the directions given by the attending psychiatrist. For example, a hospital could be liable if its attendants or nurses did not keep a patient under 24-hour supervision as ordered by a physician. Conversely, physicians might be liable if they failed to consider the notes of nurses and other staff members regarding observations of the patients.

Inpatient units are on a safer ground if they formally write out procedures for handling suicidal inpatients. Although the decision to place a patient on suicidal watch is usually within the discretion of the treating clinician, the exact procedures for the suicidal watch should conform to hospital policy. Some hospitals allow nurses the discretion to place patients on suicidal watch. Other hospitals vary as to whether a psychiatric consultation is required, whether the observer should have certain qualifications, whether there are policies for what can be included in the room, how frequent a review is required, or whether or not formal records of the observation are kept (Goldberg, 1987).

Examples have been found where a physician ordered observation of a patient, but the hospital had no written policy on what constituted observation of a patient. One nurse watched the patient constantly, but a second nurse checked the patient every 15 minutes. Apparently during the observation of the second nurse, the patient hanged herself (Perr, 1985).

Treatment plans on an outpatient basis should be adhered to carefully as well. If a suicidal patient does not comply with intensive outpatient treatment, then there may be reasons to reconsider the treatment plan and consider other treatment alternatives. Documentation of the assessment of suicide and the resulting treatment plan and its implementation are essential. A record can become either a sword for the plaintiff or a shield for the psychologist/defendant when litigation occurs.

At times patients or their families may not cooperate with the treatment recommended. In *Paddock v. Chacko* (1988), for example, a court held that a psychiatrist was not liable for the injuries suffered by a patient in an attempted suicide. The psychiatrist in North Carolina had seen the patient once and, relying on the statement of the patient that she was returning to Florida, referred her to practitioners there. When the patient called him later in a distressed state, he encouraged her to go to a hospital, which she, relying on the advice of her father, declined to do. Consequently, the court held that the psychiatrist could not be liable for the harm suffered by a patient who refused a voluntary hospitalization and who had refused follow-up outpatient treatment.

DUTY TO WARN OR PROTECT
WITH HIV-POSITIVE PATIENTS

At the start of the 21st century, more than 400,000 Americans have died from AIDS and more than 800,000 Americans are currently HIV infected. All psychotherapists should expect to experience the impact of this pandemic on their patient populations. If they have not already treated an HIV-positive patient, they probably will, or at least they will treat someone whose life has been affected by the infection.

The spread of AIDS has caused psychotherapists to ask if they are obligated to report the HIV-infection status to identifiable or readily identifiable sexual or needle-sharing partners who may be at risk for acquiring the infection. A large minority of HIV-infected persons has not disclosed their sero status to their sexual partners (Kalichman & Nachimson, 1999). However, state laws regarding reporting HIV status differ considerably from those regarding patients who threaten to assault others. For example, laws in some states prohibit psychotherapists from warning identifiable victims of persons who are HIV positive.

In those states that do not have a confidentiality statute for HIV-positive patients, the case law on a "duty to warn" with HIV-positive patients is just emerging. We were unable to find any case law dealing with psychotherapists who were held liable for failing to warn identifiable third parties. In fact, in *N.O.L. v. District of Columbia* (1995) the court ruled that the law in the District of Columbia prohibited health care providers from disclosing the HIV status of the patient to his wife.

Nonetheless, a court case finding psychotherapists liable for failure to warn an identifiable third party is conceivable in some jurisdictions. Some cases have required physicians to notify identifiable third parties of contagious diseases (see review by Bateman, 1992) and in at least one case, *Reisner v. Regents of the University of California* (1995), a physician who failed to notify a patient of her HIV status was found liable to her sexual partner who also contracted the infection from her.

CLINICAL RECOMMENDATIONS

The question of whether or not psychotherapists have an obligation to warn is legitimate, but it receives a disproportionate amount of attention. It is more important, we believe, that psychotherapists are competent to treat the patients because good clinical skills will often obviate the need to decide between warning and not warning.

Even in jurisdictions where a "duty to warn" with HIV-positive patients is legally permitted, psychotherapists need to ask themselves several questions before issuing a warning (Anderson & Barret, 2001; California Psychological Association AIDS Committee, 1994). Does the psychotherapist know an identifiable individual at risk? At times the risk may be high and the victim easily identifiable, such as when an HIV-positive patient states that he or she is having unprotected sexual relations with a partner who is unaware of the infectious status. At other times, good evidence may be lacking. There may also be instances when a lower level of verifiable risk exists, such as when a patient is having sexual relations with a live-in partner, has a history of involvement with prostitutes or other high-risk sexual partners, but has never been tested for HIV. Also, do the identifiable victims know that they are at risk? Has the psychotherapist given psychotherapy enough time to work? Does the psychotherapist understand why the patient is reluctant to disclose? Patients may elect not to disclose their status because they fear abandonment, social rejection (Kozlowski, Rupert, & Crawford, 1998), or violence.

39

We urge psychotherapists to emphasize voluntary disclosure. Attention should be given to the feelings and fears that make disclosure difficult for the patient.

Psychotherapeutic interventions have been successful in getting patients infected with HIV to reduce their high-risk behavior, thus reducing the need to warn (Franzini et al., 1990; Kelly, 1995; National Institute of Mental Health Multisite HIV Prevention Trial Group, 1998). The outcomes appear encouraging and follow ups show that progress can be sustained, although relapse should be anticipated.

Even when permitted by law, warning an identifiable third party should be used only when all reasonable efforts at a voluntary disclosure have failed. Unlike threats of violence where a single gunshot has a high likelihood of being fatal, the dangerousness of sexual contact varies according to many factors such as use of barrier contraceptives, the nature of the sexual contact, the health status of the uninfected partner, and the degree of infectiousness of the HIV-positive partner. Consequently, psychotherapists have time to give therapy a chance to work. The patient's willingness to discuss high-risk behaviors within psychotherapy may indicate concern for others that can be mobilized so that the patient will inform his or her partner voluntarily. Some strategies to facilitate voluntary disclosure may include role play, assertiveness training, or relationship enhancement.

A few patients may claim that they intend to engage in sexual activity deliberately to infect others or without regard for the possibility of disease transmission. This reaction may reflect the patient's distress with dealing with the seriousness of the disease and not represent a willful intention to harm others. Just as a verbal threat to assault a foreseeable third person may represent "blowing off steam," so the threat to infect others may reflect a temporary outburst of anger or a transient sense of nihilism brought on by learning of one's infectious status.

If the decision is made to warn an identifiable party, as when patients make a direct threat to harm themselves or others, it is prudent, if feasible, to inform the patient that the contact is going to be made and to involve the patient in the clinical decision making as much as possible. Several states have "partner notification" programs where trained state employees will notify the partners at the request of the patient. The psychotherapist or the patient can consider using the partner notification system instead of warning the intended victim directly.

MANDATORY REPORTING LAWS

Psychotherapists are often included as reporters in mandatory re-porting laws. All of these laws are based on the need to prevent harm to others and to ensure public safety. Physicians are usually required to report gunshot wounds, sexually transmitted diseases, child abuse, and (sometimes) impaired drivers. Nonmedical psychotherapists are cov-ered primarily by reporting laws for child abuse and abuse of older adults, although the older adult reporting laws are not always manda-tory.

CHILD ABUSE

Psychotherapists often encounter children who are or have been endangered by the behavior of their parents or guardians. However, child welfare advocates have succeeded in getting every state to adopt child welfare laws. These laws underwent major changes after the pas-sage of P.L. 93-247, a federal law that made federal financial assistance contingent upon certain requirements, including the mandate that cer-tain professionals report child abuse. Psychotherapists can find more details about the child protective services law in their state through the National Clearinghouse on Child Abuse and Neglect Information (http://www.calib.com/nccanch/index.html).

Child protective service laws require mental health professionals to report any suspected child abuse that they may encounter in their professional duties. The child protective service laws provide civil or criminal penalties for mandated reporters who fail to make reports as required by law. The presence of criminal sanctions for failure to report provides a strong rationale for psychologists to justify to the parents/guardians the need to make the report. Furthermore, legislators antici-pated that employers would not try to block an employee from making a report if they knew that reporting was required by law. The list of mandated reporters varies slightly from state to state, but is usually broadly worded and includes physicians, psychologists, social work-ers, mental health counselors, marriage and family therapists, teachers, and other health and social service professionals.

Most states have provisions within their licensing laws that state that the failure to fulfill a statutorily required duty is grounds for a disciplinary action. The willful or knowing failure to report suspected child abuse would qualify under this provision.

In addition to the criminal penalties, civil suits have been initiated against mandated reporters who failed to report child abuse. Several states have included provisions within their laws for civil liability for failure to report. It could be argued that these statutory provisions are redundant, however, because a civil suit could be based on simple negligence; that is, the professional could be charged with failure to adhere to the standard of care required by other similarly situated professionals.

For penalties to be applied, most state statutes require "knowing and willful failure" to report. States that have adopted this stricter standard of liability do not intend to penalize honest mistakes in interpreting ambiguous facts surrounding many child abuse cases. This is an important provision because child abuse reporting laws are often vague, and conscientious professionals may disagree on borderline cases. Consequently, criminal sanctions will likely be applied only when mandated reporters know that abuse is occurring and still fail to make a report.

On the other hand, all state laws include immunity for professionals who make reports in good faith. The underlying rationale for penalties and immunities is that the state would prefer that mandated reporters err on the side of reporting rather than risk not reporting suspicions of abuse. The immunity from prosecution for making reports should not lead psychologists to assume, however, that their treatment of families where abuse occurs involves no legal risks. Parents typically get angry when they are reported for abuse and are more willing to sue the reporter. Although a suit based on the mere fact that a report was made will be doomed to failure, angry parents may diligently seek other grounds upon which to sue.

The right of the child (or the parents acting on behalf of the child) to sue for substandard conduct is without dispute. However, a few courts have even allowed parents to sue the psychotherapists who reported them for child abuse (see for example, *Montoya by Montoya v. Bebensee*, 1988). This trend is not universal, however, and often depends upon highly unusual circumstances (Knapp & VandeCreek, 2001).

In any event, psychotherapists should know at least three important features of the child protective services law in their state: how their state defines child abuse, the conditions that activate the duty to report, and the definition of a perpetrator of child abuse.

Definition of Child Abuse. The definition of child abuse varies from state to state, but most include nonaccidental injuries, neglect, emotional abuse, and sexual abuse. Some states include promotion of prostitution and participation in pornography as child abuse. There is no substitute for knowing the exact law in one's state.

Conditions That Activate Mandated Reporting. Privileged-communication laws are typically abrogated by child abuse reporting laws. That is, a psychotherapist may not use the psychotherapist-patient privilege as a reason not to make a mandated report. However, the application of the privilege to subsequent cases following the report of the abuse varies considerably from state to state. That is, in some states privilege may protect therapy information from being accessed in subsequent court hearings regarding the child's safety. In other states, the psychotherapist may be required to testify about a child's care and safety once the report of suspected abuse has been made.

Also, in some states the duty to report under the child protective services law only applies in situations in which the child victim comes before the professional in his or her professional capacity. In other words, in some states the professional may not have a duty to report under the child protective services law if only the alleged perpetrator has come before him or her in therapy. Nevertheless, in situations in which the psychologist sees only the perpetrator, it is conceivable that the psychotherapist could be sued on the basis of the *Tarasoff* doctrine (the duty to protect) if the perpetrator revealed a credible intent to inflict serious harm to an identifiable child in the immediate future.

The threshold for making reports is low. Reporters only need to suspect (or believe) that child abuse occurred; they need not have proof. The intent of using the low threshold is that the child welfare agency and not the psychotherapist should have the responsibility to determine whether abuse actually occurred.

Definition of Perpetrators. State laws may define the term "perpetrator" differently. Every state includes the guardians or parents of the child among those who could fall under the purview of the child protective services law. Others include teachers, baby-sitters, paramours of parents, or live-in adults.

Children occasionally reveal to psychotherapists that they were harmed or abused by neighbors, older children, or casual acquaintances. These are crimes against children and can be processed through the criminal justice system, not the child welfare system. For example, if a psychotherapist treating a child learns that a noncustodial adult has abused the child, then the psychotherapist needs to discuss with the parents how to protect the child and prosecute the perpetrator. However, a report to child welfare would not be indicated because the perpetrator was not a parent, guardian, or caretaker of the child.

CLINICAL RECOMMENDATIONS

Despite the positive goals of child protective service laws, they can create a barrier to effective therapy if parents view psychotherapists as punitive agents who are required to turn them in. Psychotherapists can minimize the negative influence of these laws by informing patients of the confidentiality limitations before starting treatment. Of course, there may be nonlegal consequences to an unfounded report such as the loss of confidence between the psychotherapist and patient that may prompt the patient to discontinue psychotherapy prematurely.

It is often prudent to discuss the report with the parents, and to obtain their consent for the report when possible. If at all possible, a parent should call the child welfare agency, or the psychotherapist can call with the parent present. Although the report of abuse may harm the psychotherapeutic relationship, the effort to clarify what was done and why it was done may help to minimize any damage. Most states allow the option of reporting anonymously. This may be indicated in some situations, although patients sometimes can guess the identity of the reporter.

The mandated nature of child abuse reporting may help psychotherapists clinically in these situations. The psychotherapists can explain that the law requires them to report suspicions of child abuse and that criminal penalties can follow from a failure to do so.

As with all work with potentially dangerous patients, psychotherapists should document child abuse suspicions carefully, including the basis for the suspicions, efforts to persuade the alleged perpetrators to self-report, and attempts to keep the patient in treatment.

ABUSE OF OLDER ADULTS

The population of older Americans is growing twice as fast as all other age groups. Because of debilitating or chronic disease, many older adults receive supervision or daily support from relatives or other caregivers. Although the vast majority of these caregivers are competent and compassionate, it has been estimated that 4% of older adults are victims of elder abuse or neglect (National Center on Elder Abuse, 1998).

Most states' laws permit or require professionals to report any suspected elder abuse that they may encounter in their professional duties (Welfel, Danzinger, & Santoro, 2000). Psychotherapists should know their state's definition of elder abuse, the conditions that activate the duty to report, and the definition of a perpetrator of elder abuse. In addition, some states may mandate reporting for mental health professionals working in nursing homes or hospitals. Other states may have ombudspersons for older adults who live in long-term health care facilities. Some states include protective services for older adults under more generic statutes covering vulnerable adults.

Like child abuse reporting laws, elder abuse reporting laws typically include physical assaults, neglect, sexual abuse, or psychological abuse. In addition, elder abuse reporting laws often include financial exploitation as one of the conditions that may trigger a report. A summary of elder abuse reporting laws can be obtained from the National Center on Elder Abuse (http://www.aoa.dhhs.gov/abuse/report/default.html).

Many older adults are dependent upon their caregivers and are reluctant to come forth with their complaints. Furthermore, it may be difficult to ascertain the reliability of their complaints if they have a cognitive impairment.

Nonetheless, psychotherapists can often work within the family system to prevent such abuse from occurring in the first place. The care of older adults can be demanding and tax or exceed the capacity of the caregiver to provide the needed support. Working within the family system may reduce the tension and improve the capacity of the caregiver to respond appropriately to the needs of the older person.

IMPAIRED DRIVERS

Traffic accidents are one of the major causes of death within the United States. To reduce the frequency of such accidents, several states mandate that physicians or other health professionals report impaired drivers. Even in most states that do not have such a requirement, treating an impaired driver raises concern for the welfare of the driver and of the public. Although courts have commonly held that psychotherapists have no common law duty to the victims of accidents caused by impaired drivers, there is, nonetheless, a moral concern for these potential victims and for the patients themselves.

Psychotherapists should ask patients about driving if they appear to have neurological damage or are on sedating medications (or a combination of medications, herbal remedies, or nonprescription drugs). However, the general rule is to predict future behavior on the basis of past behavior. If patients have had accidents, or if they report that other drivers are frequently honking at them (presumably because they almost caused an accident), then an inquiry into driver impairment may be indicated. Other self-reported patient behaviors may include getting lost, not seeing oncoming traffic, or driving far slower than the flow of traffic (American Psychological Association, 1998).

Sometimes the safety of the driver depends on the person's judgment as to when to drive. Everyone knows of situations in which they (or their friends) were "too upset to drive" because of a tense emotional situation. Nonetheless, most people take the precaution of temporarily abstaining from driving. Similarly, it is often necessary to inquire as to the discretion the patients use in determining when to drive. As with dealing with patients who present an imminent danger of harming others, it is desirable to involve the patient in the decision making as much as possible. If patients resist voluntarily giving up or curtailing their driving, then it may be desirable to involve family members in decisions about driving as much as is clinically appropriate.

RISK MANAGEMENT ISSUES
WITH DANGEROUS PATIENTS

In addition to the specific standards that apply to the treatment of dangerous patients, psychotherapists need to be especially careful about other grounds of liability including abandonment; failure to consult, refer, or coordinate treatment with a physician; keeping good records; and how to respond if a suit is filed. Table 2 (p. 47) lists several questions that psychotherapists can consider when evaluating patients for dangerousness.

TABLE 2: RISK MANAGEMENT QUESTIONS

1. Do you have copies of your state/provincial or federal laws and regulations governing your practice as they pertain to the duty to protect, confidentiality with HIV-positive patients, child protective services, elder abuse, and/or impaired drivers (if any)?
2. Do you routinely ask about violence or the potential for violence when seeing patients for the first time (especially when treating marital couples)?
3. If clinically indicated, have you done a thorough evaluation of the dangerousness of the patient, including obtaining past records and interviewing significant others?

    A. Do you use a screening instrument?
    B. Do you ask detailed questions about any violent episodes in the past?
    C. Do you consider the overall mental health, life situation, and intentions of any patient before determining his or her potential for violence?

4. When patients present a threat of harming themselves or others, have you

    A. developed a treatment plan which is consistent with acceptable professional standards?
    B. considered the potential of traditional mental health treatment (intensive outpatient services or hospitalization) as opposed to an automatic assumption that a warning has to be made?
    C. implemented your treatment plan conscientiously?
    D. modified your treatment plan as circumstances change?
    E. sought clinical consultation if needed and if time permits?
    F. documented your interventions carefully, including the reasons for the actions you took? Do you ensure that your notes accurately reflect your decision-making process?
    G. notified third parties without the patient's consent if necessary to reduce the likelihood of violence?

5. When treating patients who are HIV infected, do you focus primarily on providing high quality treatment consistent with the state-of-the-art literature?
6. When patients, especially older patients, show signs of dementia, do you assess their ability to drive safely?
7. Are you careful to seek consultation when needed, coordinate treatment with other providers, and document your interventions carefully?
8. Do you take adequate measures to protect yourself both physically and mentally?
9. Do you ensure that your professional liability insurance is paid up?

AVOIDING ABANDONMENT

One fear raised by *Tarasoff* was that psychotherapists might be tempted to prematurely terminate with dangerous patients. Premature termination of treatment may place the psychotherapist at risk of a charge of legal abandonment. The legal concept of abandonment has been applied primarily in medical malpractice cases, although its extension to psychotherapy would seem logical (VandeCreek, Knapp, & Herzog, 1987). Psychotherapists in independent practice may refuse to accept potential patients into treatment for any reason, including the perceived ability of the patient to pay for services. Psychotherapists, however, do not have the unqualified right to terminate an existing relationship unless the treatment is completed, the patient ends the relationship, or the psychotherapist recommends alternative services.

The legal concept of abandonment could take one of two forms. First, abandonment would be unintentional in cases in which psychotherapists terminated or withheld treatment when they did not but should have known that further treatment was needed, and the patient suffered harm. Expert witnesses would be needed to determine the standard of reasonable care. Abandonment would be intentional in cases in which psychotherapists terminated or withheld treatment when they knew that further treatment was needed and that the patient would suffer harm. A lower standard of proof is required when a verdict of intentional abandonment is sought. The fact of termination itself, when the client clearly needed continuing care, might be sufficient to establish liability. In that case, expert witnesses would not be needed.

Despite the caution against patient abandonment, Guthiel (1985) has suggested that it can be clinically indicated to restrict or refuse an appointment with some patients at certain times. The duty to provide appointments only refers to the duty to provide clinically appropriate appointments. When psychotherapists limit or restrict appointments with impulsive or manipulative patients, they should document their treatment decision carefully to avoid the appearance of neglect.

Manipulative threats can occur among some patients with pervasive personality disorders. It is not in the interest of these patients to allow them to continue a pattern of self-defeating behaviors. The doctrine of abandonment is not intended to coerce psychotherapists into reinforcing disruptive or harmful behavior. Nonetheless, the decision to restrict appointments with these patients should be done carefully.

Even patients who engage in manipulative gestures can seriously harm or even kill themselves.

In any event, psychotherapists should never terminate treatment with patients who present a serious threat to harm themselves or others without giving (or even facilitating) a referral to an appropriate professional.

CONSULTING OR REFERRING

The duty to refer or consult arises when the psychotherapist determines, or should have determined, that the current treatments are unlikely to help the patient. This duty may become apparent in the first interview with the patient, or it may not become apparent until therapy has been conducted for many sessions.

Nonmedical psychotherapists who work with patients with serious and chronic mental disorders such as schizophrenia, manic-depressive disorders, recurrent major depression, and borderline personality disorder usually need to collaborate with a psychiatrist. Depending on the circumstances, the psychotherapist may refer the entire treatment of the patient to the physician. More often, however, the referral means continuing psychotherapy while the physician prescribes and monitors the medication.

The failure to refer patients with serious and persistent mental illnesses for medication could be grounds for malpractice. For example, in *Osheroff v. Chestnut Lodge* (1985), the patient was diagnosed as having a personality disorder and received 7 months of intensive psychodynamic psychotherapy in a hospital. His family complained about the lack of improvement and, after the hospital refused to change the treatment plan, transferred him to another hospital. There the patient responded well to medications and was discharged within 3 months. The court determined that the psychiatrists in the first hospital were negligent in their diagnosis and treatment of the patient. Expert witnesses opined that the treating psychiatrists should have modified the treatment plan when it became obvious that the patient was not responding to the intensive psychotherapy.

Liability for the patient's care typically does not extend beyond the point of referral. For example, in *Brandt v. Grubin* (1974), a physician had referred his patient for psychiatric services. The patient subsequently committed suicide, but the referring physician was not held liable. The court held that:

> A physician who upon an initial examination determines that he is incapable of helping his patient, and who refers the patient to a source of competent medical assistance, should be held liable neither for the actions of subsequent treating professionals nor for his refusal to become further involved with the case. (p. 89)

Unfortunately, some patients do not respond well to either psychotherapy or medications. Ananth (1998) reported that about 20% of patients with short-term depression are treatment resistant. When psychotherapists treat patients who do not appear to be making progress, it may be necessary to consider an underlying medical problem, rethink the diagnosis, consider pharmacological interventions, or determine if the interventions are being implemented as intended. Consultation and good documentation are especially important in these situations.

If, after doing all of these things, the psychotherapist is still unable to help the patient, then consideration should be given to discussing the prognosis candidly with the patient. This situation requires great clinical acumen. Of course, it is possible that the treatment may be preventing the patient from deteriorating further or that the patient otherwise places great value on the treatment. Any time patients show life-endangering features, psychotherapists should err on the side of recommending continued treatment either from themselves or another competent professional.

COORDINATING TREATMENT WITH PHYSICIANS

Although nonmedical psychotherapists will probably not be prescribing the medication, they can still contribute to the medical management of the patient by helping patients understand the costs and benefits of the medication, monitoring the overall state of the patient, or informing the physician of any changes in the status of the patient. In addition, the nonmedical psychotherapists should share information with the physician if the patients are self-medicating with herbal remedies or nonprescription drugs. Finally, psychotherapists should inform the prescribing physician of any suspected medication errors. Although they do not happen often, medication errors can be fatal (Fitzgerald, 1999).

There is no substitute for open communications between treating professionals. Failure to coordinate treatment could have serious consequences. This population, as a whole, is at risk for an accidental or intentional overdose (Dembling, Chen, & Vachon, 1999).

KEEPING GOOD RECORDS

Patient records serve many purposes. They help psychotherapists to monitor the quality of their treatment, recall important patient details, justify treatment to third-party payers, and ensure continuity of treatment if a patient receives subsequent services from another professional. Furthermore, a well-written record is essential in its defense against accusations of negligence. An axiom among malpractice defense attorneys is "If it isn't written down, it didn't occur."

Courts give great credence to the contents of medical records. If a statement appears in a medical record, the general assumption is that it is accurate. However, if the records do not contain essential information, then the issue can become one of credibility. That is, the psychotherapist's word as to what happened may be pitted against the word of the patient or other party.

Although state licensing laws or regulations may establish minimum requirements for recordkeeping, these minimal standards may be inadequate in the event that an allegation of misconduct is made. As it applies to life-endangering patients, it is essential that the record contain the reasons why clinical decisions were made. The conclusions in the records about patient care should be consistent with the actions of the psychotherapist. If, for example, a psychotherapist decides not to warn an identifiable third party, the record should contain the reasons why that decision was made. It would not be desirable to have the record contain all the reasons why a warning should be made, but then have the psychotherapist fail to make such a warning.

RESPONDING TO A SUIT

Psychotherapists need to act with due discretion when a suit is threatened. As it applies to life-endangering patients, lawsuits are typically threatened or filed after patients have already harmed themselves or another person.

Whenever a patient or third party has hired an attorney to pursue the complaint, psychotherapists should notify their malpractice insurance carrier and contact an attorney. The issues are no longer clinical ones in which the psychotherapist needs to be proactive. It is now a legal issue in which the psychotherapist has the potential to suffer serious professional consequences. Psychotherapists should take no actions on the case at these times without consulting their attorney first.

SELF-CARE

Self-care refers to the efforts of psychotherapists to protect or enhance their physical or mental well-being. The same moral principle of beneficence that requires psychotherapists to promote the welfare of their patients also dictates that psychotherapists have a moral responsibility to care for themselves as well. Self-care has a utilitarian aspect to it as well; it is necessary to function well emotionally in order to be an effective psychotherapist. This section reviews ways that psychotherapists can protect themselves both physically and emotionally from the challenges of dealing with dangerous patients.

PATIENTS WHO THREATEN PSYCHOTHERAPISTS

At some time in their careers, many psychotherapists will be assaulted, threatened, or stalked by patients. Although it may not be possible for psychotherapists to screen all such patients over the phone, as much as possible they can simply refuse to take patients whom they believe may threaten them personally.

Also, psychotherapists need to take precautions with patients who present themselves as threatening. First, they can ensure that they are not alone in the office with such patients by only scheduling those patients at busy times as opposed to the end of the day. Even if they are alone, they can structure their offices so that they have an easy escape to the door, can easily reach the telephone for help, or have other structural safety advantages. Having a security system with an alarm installed may be warranted. There is no substitute for having basic information about nonviolent techniques for diffusing violent patients (see Tishler, Gordon, & Landry-Meyer, 2000).

If a patient threatens or intimidates the psychotherapist, then the psychotherapist needs to determine if this can be handled therapeutically. It may be necessary to establish limits on what is or is not acceptable, or to explore transference or countertransference issues.

If an assault or another crime does occur, criminal charges against the patient might be appropriate if psychotherapists have exhausted their therapeutic options with the patient and the patient appears capable of distinguishing acceptable from unacceptable behavior. In making the final decision about whether or not to prosecute a patient, psychotherapists should consider the degree of internal control of the patient, the probability that the patient will repeat the violence or the threat, the willingness of the courts to prosecute, and the probable effect on the patient in the long term. For some patients, especially those with treatment-resistant personality disorders, prosecution may instill an understanding of the need for limits on their behavior. For other patients, such prosecutions would be clinically contraindicated and do little to further the safety of the psychotherapist or society in general. Because psychotherapists who treat threatening patients often have to address countertransference reactions, consultations may be especially helpful.

EMOTIONAL SELF-CARE

Throughout their careers, psychotherapists can expect to encounter suicides or attempted suicides of their patients, patient threats to third persons, and other situations which may not be life-endangering but which are nonetheless very upsetting. Self-care requires psychotherapists to protect themselves emotionally as well as physically. Few events can be as disturbing as having patients harming themselves or others.

In their review of the literature on the impact of patient emergencies on clinicians, Kleespies and Dettmer (2000) found that 46% of psychiatrists had a patient commit suicide and between 22% and 29% of psychologists had a patient commit suicide. In addition, in a 1-year period, 81% of psychologists reported a fear that a patient might harm another person. Very often psychotherapists develop clinical depression or other emotional disorders following these upsetting events.

Psychotherapists need to be prepared for these challenges. Although these stressful life events and circumstances are difficult to manage, psychotherapists can reduce the likelihood of occurrence or, at least, to ameliorate the impact if they do occur.

First, psychotherapists can anticipate that such violent events can occur. Psychotherapists should always keep in the back of their minds that their patients may harm others or themselves. With this mind-set, psychotherapists are more likely to ask the pertinent questions and to take necessary clinical precautions when dealing with patients.

Also, few resources can be as helpful as that of a strong social support network. Sharing the burden has both clinical and personal benefits. Clinically, those psychologists who receive regular consultation from others will benefit from their shared clinical expertise, be able to deliver a higher standard of care and, consequently, be better at assessing danger and better at developing and implementing treatment plans to diffuse that danger. Also, sharing the burden has psychological benefits as well. Just the opportunity to express one's dismay can have healing effects and reduce the stress inherent in having to make a difficult decision where the right answer is not always clear.

Finally, if the unfortunate event of a patient suicide or homicide does occur, then it will be important for the psychotherapist to receive emotional support or even enter into psychotherapy if necessary. The self-care for such an event also means attending to the legal complications that may arise. In the event of such an occurrence, there is no substitute for seeking competent legal advice. It furthers no moral end for a psychotherapist who functioned competently to undergo a lengthy civil suit arising out of an unforeseeable or unpreventable tragedy.

SUMMARY

Some psychotherapists and scholars have feared that the duty to protect court cases and related statutes would severely limit therapeutic options in the treatment of dangerous patients. We have seen no evidence to support this worry. Rather, good clinical practice continues to be the best risk management strategy for the management of dangerous patients.

This guidebook has presented the *Tarasoff* decision in detail along with other subsequent court cases and statutory rules to assist psychotherapists in managing several types of dangerous patients. Our goal has not been to provide a comprehensive treatment guidebook, but rather to focus more on the legal and ethical considerations that should be integrated into clinical care.

There is no substitute for knowledge of one's local, state, and federal laws and regulations that impact on patient care.

REFERENCES

American Law Institute. (1966). *Restatement of the Law, Second, Torts.* St. Paul, MN: American Law Institute Publishers.

American Psychological Association. (1998). *Older Adults' Health and Age-Related Changes: Reality Versus Myth.* Washington, DC: Author.

Analyst found culpable in sexual molestation case. (1998, November 6). *Psychiatric News, 14,* 18.

Ananth, J. (1998). Treatment resistant depression. *Psychotherapy and Psychosomatics, 67,* 61-70.

Anderson, J., & Barret, R. (Eds.). (2001). *Ethics in HIV-Related Psychotherapy: Clinical Decision Making in Complex Cases.* Washington, DC: American Psychological Association.

Appelbaum, P. (1985). *Tarasoff* and the clinician: Problems in fulfilling the duty to protect. *American Journal of Psychiatry, 142,* 429.

Bateman, T. A. (1992). Liability of doctor or other health practitioner to third party contracting contagious disease from doctor's patient. *American Law Reports, 3, ALR 5th,* 370-393.

Beauchamp, T., & Childress, J. (1994). *Principles of Biomedical Ethics* (4th ed.). New York: Oxford.

Beauford, J., McNiel, D., & Binder, R. (1997). Utility of the initial therapeutic alliance in evaluating psychiatric patients' risk of violence. *American Journal of Psychiatry, 154,* 1272-1276.

Beigler, J. S. (1984). Tarasoff v. confidentiality. *Behavioral Sciences & the Law, 2,* 273-288.

Binder, R., & McNiel, D. (1996). Application of the *Tarasoff* ruling and its effect on the victim and the therapeutic relationship. *Psychiatric Services, 47,* 1212-1215.

Bongar, B., Maris, R., Berman, S. L., & Litman, F. E. (1992). Outpatient standards of care in the assessment, management and treatment of suicidal persons. *Suicide and Life Threatening Behavior, 22*(4), 453-478.

Bonner, R. (1992). Suicide prevention in correctional facilities. In L. VandeCreek, S. Knapp, & T. L. Jackson (Eds.), *Innovations in Clinical Practice: A Source Book* (Vol. 11, pp. 467-480). Sarasota, FL: Professional Resource Press.

Borum, R. (2000). Assessing violence risk among youths. *Journal of Clinical Psychology, 58,* 1263-1286.

Bradley Center v. Wessner, 287 S.E.2d 716 (Ga. App. 1982).

Brandt v. Grubin, 329 A.2d 82 (N.J. Super. 1974).

Brown, G., Beck, A. T., Steer, R., & Grisham, J. (2000). Risk factors for suicide in psychiatric outpatients: A 20 year prospective study. *Journal of Consulting and Clinical Psychology, 68,* 371-377.

Bruni, F. (1998, April 19). Child psychiatrist and pedophile: His therapist knew but didn't tell: A victim is suing. *New York Times*, pp. 35, 40.

California Psychological Association AIDS Committee. (1994, December). Confidentiality and prevention of HIV transmission. *California Psychologist*, pp. 17, 21.

Carlino v. State, 294 N.Y.S.2d 30 (1968).

Clarke, E. C. (2000). Will recent progress in limiting use continue? *Behavioral Health Tomorrow, 9*(3), 30-32.

Cole v. Taylor, 301 N.W.2d 766 (Iowa 1981).

Comiskey v. State of New York, 418 N.Y.S.2d 233 (1979).

Dalton v. State, 308 N.Y.S.2d 441 (Sup. Ct. N.Y. App. 1970).

Darren v. Safier, 615 N.Y.S.2nd 926 (A.D. 2 Dept. 1994).

Dembling, B., Chen, D., & Vachon, L. (1999). Life expectancy and causes of death in a population treated for serious mental illness. *Psychiatric Services, 50,* 1036-1042.

Dinnerstein v. United States, 486 F.2d 34 (1973).

Doby v. DeCrescenzo, 171 F.3rd 858 (3d Cir. 1999).

Douglas, K., Ogloff, J., Nicholls, T., & Grant, I. (1999). Assessing risk for violence among psychiatric patients. The HCR-20 Violence Risk Assessment Scheme and the Psychopathology Checklist: Screening Version. *Journal of Consulting and Clinical Psychology, 67,* 917-930.

Emerich v. Philadelphia Center for Human Development, 720 A.2d 1032 (Pa. 1998).

Fair v. United States, 234 F.2d 288 (5th Cir. 1956).

Fitzgerald, W. (1999). Legal and ethical considerations in the treatment of psychosis. *Journal of Clinical Psychiatry, 60*(Suppl. 19), 59-63.

Franzini, J., Sideman, L., Dexter, K., & Elder, J. (1990). Promoting AIDS risk reduction via behavioral training. *AIDS Education and Prevention, 2,* 313-321.

Goldberg, R. (1987). Use of constant observation with potentially suicidal patients in general hospitals. *Hospital and Community Psychiatry, 38,* 303-305.

Greenberg v. Barbour, 322 F. Supp. 745 (D. Pa. 1971).

Guthiel, T. (1985). Medicolegal pitfalls in the treatment of borderline patients. *American Journal of Psychotherapy, 142,* 914.

Hare, R. (1991). *Manual for the Hare Psychopathology Checklist: Revised.* Toronto, Canada: Multi-Health Systems.

Harris, G. T., & Quincy, V. (1993). Violent recidivism of mentally disordered offenders: The development of a statistical prediction instrument. *Criminal Justice and Behavior, 20,* 315-335.

Hedlund v. Superior Court of Orange County, 669 P.2d 41, 191 Cal. Rptr. 805 (1983).

Hicks v. United States, 511 F.2d 407 (D.C. Cir. 1975).

Hirsch v. State, 168 N.E.2d 372 (1960).

Hofmann v. Blackmon, 241 So.2d 752 (Fla. App. 1970).

Huber, M., Balon, R., Labbate, L., Brandt-Youtz, S., Hammer, J., & Mufti, R. (2000). A survey of police officers' experience with Tarasoff warnings in two states. *Psychiatric Services, 51,* 807-809.

Illinois v. Ranstrom. (1999, May/June). *Mental Disability Law Reporter, 23*(3), 321.

Jablonski v. United States, 712 F.2d 391 (9th Cir. 1983).

Jenks v. Brown, 557 N.W.2d 114 (Mich. Ct. App. 1996).

Jury faults Ga. psychologist in duty-to-warn case. (2000, March 3). *Psychiatric News,* pp. 11, 32.

Kaiser v. Suburban Transportation System, 65 Wash.2d 461, 398 P.2d 14 (1965).

Kalichman, S., & Nachimson, D. (1999). Self-efficacy and disclosure of HIV-positive serostatus to sex partners. *Health Psychology, 18,* 281-287.

Kamenar, P. D. (1984). Psychiatrist's duty to warn of a dangerous patient: A survey of the law. *Behavioral Sciences & the Law, 2,* 259-272.

Kelly, J. (1995). *Changing HIV Risk Behavior: Practical Strategies.* New York: Guilford.

King, J. (1977). *The Law of Medical Malpractice.* St. Paul, MN: West.

Kleespies, P., & Dettmer, E. (2000). The stress of patient emergencies for the clinician: Incidence, impact and means of coping. *Journal of Clinical Psychology, 56,* 1352-1369.

Knapp, S., & VandeCreek, L. (1983). Malpractice risks with suicidal patients. *Psychotherapy: Theory, Research and Practice, 20,* 274-280.

Knapp, S., & VandeCreek, L. (1987). A review of tort liability in involuntary civil commitment. *Hospital and Community Psychiatry, 38,* 648-651.

Knapp, S., & VandeCreek, L. (2001). *The Duty to Third Parties: Does It Extend to Alleged Perpetrators of Child Abuse?* Manuscript submitted for publication.

Kozlowski, N., Rupert, P., & Crawford, I. (1998). Psychotherapy with HIV-infected clients: Factors influencing notification of third parties. *Psychotherapy, 35,* 105-115.

Leonard, J. B. (1977). A therapist's duty to potential victims: A non-threatening view of Tarasoff. *Law and Human Behavior, 1,* 309-317.

Lidz, C., Mulvey, E., & Gardner, W. (1993). The accuracy of predictions of violence to others. *Journal of the American Medical Association, 269,* 1007-1011.

Malone, K., Oquendo, M., Haas, G., Ellis, S., Li, S., & Mann, J. J. (2000). Protective factors against suicidal acts in major depression: Reasons for living. *American Journal of Psychiatry, 157,* 1084-1088.

Matter of Estate of Votteler, 327 N.W. 759 (Iowa 1982).

McCarthy, M. (1964). *The Group.* New York: Signet.

McNamara v. Honeyman, 546 N.E.2d 139 (Mass. Sup. Jud. Co. 1989).

McNiel, D., Binder, R., & Fulton, F. (1998). Management of threats of violence under California's duty-to-protect statute. *American Journal of Psychiatry, 155,* 1097-1101.

Medicare and Medicaid programs: Hospital conditions of participation. (1999, July 2). *Federal Register, 64,* 36069-36089.

Meloy, J. R. (1997). The clinical risk management of stalking: "Someone is watching over me. . . ." *American Journal of Psychotherapy, 51,* 174-184.

Menzies, R., Webster, C. D., & Sepejak, D. (1985). The dimensions of dangerousness: Evaluating the accuracy of psychometric predictions of violence among forensic patients. *Law and Human Behavior, 9,* 35-56.

Monahan, J. (1993). Limiting therapist exposure to *Tarasoff* liability: Guidelines for risk containment. *American Psychologist, 48,* 242-250.

Monahan, J., & Steadman, H. (1996). Violent storms and violent people: How meteorology can inform risk communication in mental health law. *American Psychologist, 51,* 931-938.

Monahan, J., Steadman, H., Appelbaum, P., Robbins, P., Mulvey, E., Silver, E., Roth, L., & Grisso, T. (2000). Developing a clinically useful actuarial tool for assessing risk. *British Journal of Psychiatry, 176,* 312-319.

Montoya by Montoya v. Bebensee, 761 P.2d 285 (Colo. Ct. App. 1988).

Moore v. United States, 222 F. Supp. 87 (D. Mo. 1963).

National Center on Elder Abuse. (1998). *National Elder Abuse Incidence Study: Final Report* [On-line]. Available: http://www.aoa.dhhs.gov/abuse/report/default.html

National Clearinghouse on Child Abuse and Neglect Information. Website: http://www.calib.com/nccanch/index.html

National Institute of Mental Health (NIMH) Multisite HIV Prevention Trial Group. (1998). The NIMH multisite HIV prevention trial: Reducing HIV sexual risk behavior. *Science, 280,* 1889-1894.

N.O.L. v. District of Columbia, 674 A.2d 498 (D.C. 1995).

Osheroff v. Chestnut Lodge, 490 A.2d 720 (Md. App. 1985).

O'Sullivan v. Presbyterian Hospital, 634 N.Y.S.2d 101 (A.D. 1 Dept. 1995).

Otto, R. (2000). Assessing and managing violence risk in outpatient settings. *Journal of Clinical Psychology, 56,* 1239-1262.

Paddock v. Chacko, 522 So.2d 410 (Fla. App. 5 Dist. 1988).

Paradies v. Benedictine Hospital, 431 N.Y.S.2d 175 (App. Div. 1980).

Peck v. The Counseling Service of Addison County, 499 A.2d 422 (Vt. 1985).

Perr, I. (1985). Suicide litigation and risk management: A review of 32 cases. *Bulletin of the American Academy of Psychiatry and Law, 13,* 209-219.

Prosser, W., & Keaton, W. (1985). *Prosser and Keaton on the Law of Torts.* St. Paul: West.

Reisner v. Regents of the University of California, 31 Cal. App. 4th 1195 (Cal. Ct. App. 1995).

Riggs, D., Caufield, M., & Street, A. (2000). Risk for domestic violence: Factors associated with perpetration and victimization. *Journal of Clinical Psychology, 56,* 1289-1316.

Schlegel v. New Milford Hospital. (2000, July/August). *Mental Disability Law Reporter, 24,* 646.

Seligman, M. (1989). Research in clinical psychology: Why is there so much depression today? In I. Cohen (Ed.), *The G. Stanley Hall Lecture Series* (Vol. 9, pp. 75-96). Washington, DC: American Psychological Association.

Simon, R. (2000). Taking the "sue" out of suicide: A forensic psychiatrist's perspective. *Psychiatric Annals, 30,* 399-407.

Skillings v. Allen, 173 N.W. 663 (Minn. 1919).

Stone, A. (1976). The Tarasoff decision: Suing psychotherapists to safeguard society. *Harvard Law Review, 90,* 358-378.

Swartz, M., Swanson, J., Hiday, V., Borum, R., Wagner, H. R., & Burns, B. (1998). Violence and mental illness: The effects of substance abuse and nonadherence to medication. *American Journal of Psychiatry, 1551,* 226-231.

Tarasoff v. Regents of the University of California, 13 Cal.3d 177, 529 P.2d 533 (1974), *vacated,* 17 Cal.3d 425, 551 P.2d 334 (1976).

Tarasoff warning does not waive psychotherapy privilege, judge rules. (2000, October 20). *Psychiatric News,* p. 2.

Tardiff, K., & Koenigsburg, H. W. (1985). Assaultive behavior among psychiatric outpatients. *American Journal of Psychiatry, 142,* 960-963.

Teasley v. United States, 662 F.2d 787 (D.D.C. 1980).

Thapar v. Zezulka, 994 S.W.2d 635 (Tex. Sup. Ct. 1999).

Tishler, C., Gordon, L., & Landry-Meyer, L. (2000). Managing the violent patient: A guide for psychologists and other mental health professionals. *Professional Psychology: Research and Practice, 31,* 34-41.

Truscott, D., Evans, J., & Mansell, S. (1995). Outpatient psychotherapy with dangerous clients: A model for clinical decision making. *Professional Psychology: Research and Practice, 26,* 484-490.

Underwood v. United States, 356 F.2d 92 (5th Cir. 1966).

VandeCreek, L., Knapp, S., & Herzog, C. (1987). Malpractice risks in the treatment of dangerous patients. *Psychotherapy, 24,* 145-153.

Viviano v. Moan, 645 So.2nd 1301 (La. App. 4th Cir. 1994).

Webster, C. D., Douglas, K., Eaves, D., & Hart, S. (1997). *HCR-20: Assessing Risk for Violence, Version 2.* Burnaby, BC: Mental Health, Law, and Policy Institute, Simon Fraser University.

Welfel, E. R., Danzinger, P., & Santoro, S. (2000). Mandated reporting of abuse/maltreatment of older adults: A primer for counselors. *Journal of Counseling and Development, 78,* 284-292.

Wojcik v. Aluminum Company of America, 183 N.Y.S.2d 351 (1959).

EARN 3 HOME STUDY CONTINUING EDUCATION CREDITS*

Professional Resource Exchange, Inc. offers a 3-credit home study continuing education program as a supplement to this book. For information, please return this form, call 1-800-443-3364, fax to 941-343-9201, write to the address below, or visit our website: http://www.prpress.com

Name: _____
(Please Print)

Address: _____

Address: _____

City/State/Zip: _____
This is ☐ home ☐ office

Telephone: (_____) _____

E-mail: _____

I am a:

☐ Psychologist   ☐ Mental Health Counselor
☐ Psychiatrist   ☐ Marriage and Family Therapist
☐ School Psychologist   ☐ Other: _____
☐ Clinical Social Worker

Professional Resource Press
P.O. Box 15560
Sarasota, FL 34277-1560

Telephone: 800-443-3364
FAX: 941-343-9201
E-mail: mail@prpress.com
Website: http://www.prpress.com

TAB3/7/01(ETHICS)

Add A Colleague To Our Mailing List . . .

If you would like us to send our latest catalog to one of your colleagues, please return this form:

Name: _____
(Please Print)

Address: _____

Address: _____

City/State/Zip: _____
This is ❒ home ❒ office

Telephone: (_____)_____

E-mail: _____

This person is a:

❒ Psychologist   ❒ Mental Health Counselor
❒ Psychiatrist   ❒ Marriage and Family Therapist
❒ School Psychologist   ❒ Other: _____
❒ Clinical Social Worker

Person completing this form: _____

◆   ◆   ◆

Professional Resource Press
P.O. Box 15560
Sarasota, FL 34277-1560

Telephone: 800-443-3364
FAX: 941-343-9201
E-mail: mail@prpress.com
Website: http://www.prpress.com

TAB3/7/01(ETHICS)

EARN 3 HOME STUDY CONTINUING EDUCATION CREDITS*

Professional Resource Exchange, Inc. offers a 3-credit home study continuing education program as a supplement to this book. For information, please return this form, call 1-800-443-3364, fax to 941-343-9201, write to the address below, or visit our website: http://www.prpress.com

Name: _____
(Please Print)

Address: _____

Address: _____

City/State/Zip: _____
This is ☐ home ☐ office

Telephone: (_____)_____

E-mail: _____

I am a:

☐ Psychologist   ☐ Mental Health Counselor
☐ Psychiatrist   ☐ Marriage and Family Therapist
☐ School Psychologist   ☐ Other: _____
☐ Clinical Social Worker

Professional Resource Press
P.O. Box 15560
Sarasota, FL 34277-1560

Telephone: 800-443-3364
FAX: 941-343-9201
E-mail: mail@prpress.com
Website: http://www.prpress.com

Add A Colleague To Our Mailing List . . .

If you would like us to send our latest catalog to one of your colleagues, please return this form:

Name: _____
(Please Print)

Address: _____

Address: _____

City/State/Zip: _____
This is ☐ home ☐ office

Telephone: (_____)_____

E-mail: _____

This person is a:

☐ Psychologist   ☐ Mental Health Counselor
☐ Psychiatrist   ☐ Marriage and Family Therapist
☐ School Psychologist   ☐ Other: _____
☐ Clinical Social Worker

Person completing this form: _____

◆   ◆   ◆

Professional Resource Press
P.O. Box 15560
Sarasota, FL 34277-1560

Telephone: 800-443-3364
FAX: 941-343-9201
E-mail: mail@prpress.com
Website: http://www.prpress.com